CONSUMER GUIDE TO

ADOPTING A CHILD

EVERYTHING YOU NEED TO KNOW FOR A SUCCESSFUL ADOPTION

CONSUMER GUIDE TO

ADOPTING A CHILD

EVERYTHING YOU NEED TO KNOW FOR A SUCCESSFUL ADOPTION

ROBERT A. KASKY

AND

JEFFREY A. KASKY

Cover design by Tony Nuccio

Printed in the United States of America.

20 19 18 17 16   5 4 3 2 1

Library of Congress Cataloging-in-Publication Data
Names: Kasky, Robert A., author. | Kasky, Jeffrey A., author.
Title: The ABA consumer guide to adopting a child : everything you need to
    know for a successful adoption / Robert A. Kasky and Jeffrey A. Kasky.
Description: Chicago : American Bar Association, 2015. | Includes index.
Identifiers: LCCN 2015043391 (print) | LCCN 2015044601 (ebook) | ISBN
    9781634250238 (softcover : alk. paper) | ISBN 9781634250245 ()
Subjects: LCSH: Adoption—Law and legislation—United States—Popular works.
    | Adoptive parents—United States—Handbooks, manuals, etc.
Classification: LCC KF545 .K373 2015 (print) | LCC KF545 (ebook) | DDC
    346.7301/78—dc23
LC record available at http://lccn.loc.gov/2015043391

Discounts are available for books ordered in bulk. Special consideration is given to state bars, CLE programs, and other bar-related organizations. Inquire at Book Publishing, ABA Publishing, American Bar Association, 321 N. Clark Street, Chicago, Illinois 60654-7598.

www.ShopABA.org

Dedication

This book is dedicated to the courageous men and women on the front lines of the adoption field. While they are often thanked profusely, only their colleagues know the true toll taken by the work in this field.

Contents

Acknowledgments

Robert would like to thank:

Thanks to my grandchildren Julian, Cameron, Jack, Holden, Jamie, and Connor (in order of age, of course!), who inspire me every day.

Jeff would like to thank:

Thank you first and foremost to my family: My putative father/law partner Robert Kasky and my mother Nancy Kasky, without whom I literally wouldn't be here; my sister Jill, who to this day still insists that she is an only child, and Michael, Jack, and Jamie; my children Julian, Cameron, Holden, and Connor, the coolest kids on earth and the reason I will enjoy helping people for the rest of my natural life, and possibly then some; and my awesome fiancée Jeannette, who is simply the most patient person I know.

Thank you to Margaret T. Snider, MSW, the one and only Executive Director One World Adoption Services has ever had and a contributor to this book by virtue of having been involved in every single adoption I have ever had the honor of working on; to the team members at One World who have supported Marge's, my father's, and my efforts to help people for all these years, including but

not limited to Paula Ostroviesky, Estela Euceda, Jan Zuza, Alice Kasky, Leslie Levine, Maureen Bennett, Jessica Charbonneau, Jennifer Snyder, Juliana Triana, Suzanne Ludwig, Trina Augello, Roseangela Santos, Cece, Tonya, and anyone I neglected to mention.

Thank you to The Autism Channel, Inc., for bringing free quality programming to the autism community. Thank you to Life Through Surrogacy, Inc., run by the aforementioned Jeannette, who is working hard every day to help people realize their dream of becoming parents.

Thank you to all of the judges and clerks who have supported our work by being there to do their part.

Thank you to the editors and hard-working publicists at the American Bar Association for knowing there would be an audience in need of the information we present herein.

And last but certainly not least, thank you to all of the adoptive families who trusted us to help them create their families, and who've taken such good care of the kids we've entrusted to their care!

Introduction

Congratulations. You are considering the possibility of adopting a child. If you are like most prospective adoptive parents, you're hopeful, eager, and nervous. You dream of providing a loving and supportive home to a child. At the same time, you may be concerned about the intricacies of the adoption process. And, you may wonder whether the child you adopt will prove to be a good match with your family. You're willing to take that risk, and for that we commend you.

There are many varieties of adoptions, and, while there are many similarities in each approach, there are nuances in each that prospective parents should understand. You, the reader, should know that the authors of this book have, at the time of its writing, close to 70 collective years' experience in the area of private adoption in the state of Florida. We have handled many cases with interstate aspects, and we have worked many times with the state's child welfare agencies to assist children in the "public" welfare system foster care. However, the overwhelming majority of our experience is in private attorney adoptions and private agency adoptions.

That said, you should take solace in the fact that many, if not most, of the overriding concepts of adoption are similar, as between "private" and "public" adoptions, and from state to state.

A word on gender. We make every effort to be gender neutral where appropriate. Adoptees can be he or she, his or her. Birth mothers, however, are always female, and birth fathers are always male.

It's easy to get hung up on the singular-versus-plural issue with both birth and adoptive parents. The fact is that sometimes it's one and sometimes it's two. We'll do our best to put that (s) where appropriate, but rest assured we're cognizant, respectful, and understanding of the fact that families come in all shapes, sizes, and varieties. This includes same-sex couples, of course, be they married or otherwise.

Please also note that this book was written by two authors. Each, for the most part, agrees with the other's take or perspective on things. There are no fundamental disagreements being played out in the pages herein. Believe me, there's plenty of drama even without that! When the collective pronouns "we" or "us" are used, you can safely assume that we're both speaking with you. However, some of the content herein is comprised of stories describing actual nonfictional scenarios that have played out over the years. When one or the other of us is imparting an experience to you via one of these stories, it is likely that the other wasn't there for it. Therefore, singular pronouns might be used. We hope this doesn't create undue confusion.

Honesty. Such a lonely word. This manuscript is not being created to deliver false information or to "candy-coat" the truth. We intend to give you the truth, and you might not like it. Neither of your authors is trying to make friends, we just want you to know the truth.

There are plenty of adoption books out there that include holding hands and singing Kumbaya. This is not one of them. Our intent is to provide you with the unvarnished truth about adoptions and the risks involved for all parties. The truth is that sometimes ugly things happen in adoption proceedings and you, as prospective adoptive parents, should be aware of what can go wrong. That said, we've been involved in well over 1,500 successful adoptions. Knowing the potential pitfalls will increase your chances of participating in your own success story.

The Goals of the Book

There are few areas of the law which pack as emotional a punch as adoption. Its impact is, among others, emotional, societal, social, familial, and financial. The goal of this book is to give readers insight into this potentially life-changing process and to deliver a balanced picture of this field of law as it applies, primarily, to a prospective adoptive family which desires to adopt a young or newborn child. That is the phase of the adoption process which is most interesting, turbulent, and variable. As you will see, it is obvious that this book should not be considered anything even remotely related to a legal treatise; it is intended to be consumer-oriented.

To a lesser extent, there is some attention paid herein to older-child, relative (i.e., grandparent)

and stepparent and foster parent adoptions; but the emphasis herein is on the process of adopting a newborn child. It should also be noted that this book does not delve deeply into the issues which surround *contested* adoptions as it is intended to be a general guide to the aspects of adoption which are likely to be experienced by the most people.

Since the coauthors are Florida attorneys who represent and sit on the Board of Directors of a Florida–licensed not-for-profit child-placing agency, there will be a heavy tilt toward Florida laws, procedures, rules, and regulations. The book aims, nevertheless, to give the reader a generalized view of the numerous pieces of the adoption puzzle which apply to all adoptions.

Along with the information which we think you will need to carefully consider, we have interspersed herein several stories inspired by actual events to both inform and entertain you. Some of the stories will bring a chuckle, some an "aha" moment, and others a tear to your eyes. All of these stories are 100% *true* (names changed of course), and each carries what we hope will be a valuable point to the reader.

One of our goals is to make this book "conversational" rather than an endless stream of legal citations and footnotes. Please remember as you read on that every state has different and unique laws governing and regulating adoptions and, therefore, if you are in the adoption mode, you must become informed of your state's laws. The best way to proceed, of course, is to seek professional and knowledgeable legal counsel in your geographical area. I think we've made that point.

Disclaimer

The authors of this book are lawyers, but we're not *your* lawyers. Nothing involved with the purchase or consumption of this manuscript creates a legal relationship between the authors and the readers. "Advice" given herein is not being given in the legal sense of the word; it's merely anecdotal. In fact, the authors seriously suggest to the point where we practically *insist* that if you're interested in pursuing an adoption, you find and engage an experienced lawyer.

How do you find an experienced lawyer? You ask around, perhaps to those who have had positive experiences in the same process in which you're interested (presumably adoption), and/or visit your state's bar website. That said, nothing beats a personal referral, as far as we're concerned.

Furthermore, we're not just lawyers, we're *Florida* lawyers. Each state has its own statues, rules, processes, and procedures as to how adoptions are handled. Sometimes those procedures differ from jurisdiction to jurisdiction even within a single state! What we say regarding a Florida case may be very, very different for the same case in a different state.

Also, keep in mind that the outcome of any given case – be it adoption or otherwise – is often driven by very specific facts, along with the way in which those facts are interpreted by various parties, not least of which is the trier of fact, such as the judge or jury. Any case which we discuss herein is subject to interpretation, and as we know there are many shades of gray.

You may also notice that we have included some very basic and generic "forms," simply as an example of what they sometimes look like. Once again, the field of adoption is so fact-specific that forms should only be used as conceptual guidelines, and are only provided herein as examples. You are free to petition your court in the way you see most fit. With that said, the corners you cut by trying to do something as technical as adoption on your own and without experienced counsel can, in many cases, come back to haunt you. When an adoption case haunts you, *it really haunts you*, so think long and hard about how you wish to proceed.

The Florida Bar would probably want me to clarify the fact that this is not a solicitation. We are not seeking to represent you as your lawyers, nor are we offering our services to you. Nonetheless, we'd be honored to speak at your organization's function if you'd like to have us, but as presenters, not your legal counsel. We have also been used as expert witnesses in a variety of different types of adoption-related litigation, including the emerging tort of "wrongful adoption." Lastly, we are regularly engaged to mediate adoption-related cases. Sometimes the mediation is between prospective adoptive parents and a biological parent who is asserting parental rights and opposing the adoption. Sometimes there is a post-adoption contact plan in place and one party or the other is having trouble with the other side's compliance. We understand these issues and their genesis, and have had success in helping with these cases.

Adoption Basics

We can all agree that every child deserves to start his or her life out in the best possible circumstances to fit his or her situation. "Permanence" is the word and concept which is often used to describe the situation wherein a child is adopted and made a legal part of a family. Adoption is one of several legal alternatives to the biological creation of a family to help accomplish the goal of giving a child a good start in life.

By definition, "adoption" is a state-legislated legal process that enables a parent–child relationship to be created where there was none. Adoption is often accomplished between people who have no biological connection; however, certainly adoptions are available and often completed between family members.

The legal effect of a completed adoption process is that the person being adopted (sometimes referred to as the "adoptee") becomes the legal child of the adoptive parent(s). The adoptive parents acquire all rights, duties, and responsibilities of parenthood with respect to the adoptee who, depending on his or her age, may thus become entitled to be supported emotionally and financially as if he or she was a biological child of the adoptive parents. In fact, should there be a death, divorce, or separation of or between the adoptive parents, the adoptee is entitled to be considered as a biological child for the purposes of inheritance, child support, visitation as well as all other aspects that apply to the death of a biological parent or the legal dissolution of a marriage.

Of course, the primary and "public policy" goal of adoption is to provide and promote the welfare of children and to do what's in the best interests of children when adoption meets that criterion. With this as the focal point, the process also gives comfort to the birth parents that the children whom they created are in permanent, stable families, that the various relevant government entities know that the

An adopted child has exactly the same rights as a biological child, including rights regarding inheritance, child support, and visitation.

children's welfare and best interests are being addressed, and that the children in most cases will not require government assistance.

There is neither a constitutional nor other legal right to be a parent nor is there a law that says you *must* be a parent. Thus, some couples who have tried to create a family the "usual" way and have been unsuccessful in doing so find the fact that they have to go through the often risky and complicated process of adoption in order to become parents fundamentally unfair. Others determine that it's "not meant to be" and go about their lives without becoming parents. Adoption agencies and lawyers do not have a legal responsibility to create parents out of everyone who is determined to take that route. For the most part, and within reason, lawyers and agencies can pick and choose the clients with whom they want to work.

Further, there are laws that restrict those who can adopt, and such laws require a prospective adoptive family to jump through some hoops to qualify for adoption. For instance, most, but not all, adoptions require prospective adoptive parents to have FBI background checks and clearances, local law enforcement checks and clearances, child-abuse checks and clearances, and detailed and comprehensive home studies both before and after the birth and placement of the child with a prospective adoptive family. Failure to adhere to strict regulations and complete a thorough investigation can cost an agency its license or worse.

At the end of the day, it is a judge in a court with jurisdiction over the adoption who will be asked to rule on and execute a final judgment of adoption.

There is no fundamental right to adoption. Prospective adoptive parents must go through an extensive background check and evaluation. Some prospective adopters are rejected by a judge and some decide to give up owing to the stringency and complexity of the legal process.

When properly completed, the adoption process terminates the parental rights of the adoptee's biological parents and creates a new legal relationship the effect of which is to make the adoptee the legal child of the adoptive family as if the child was born into that family.

The best interests of the child are paramount throughout the process. By the same token, the interests of the birth parents, the adoptive parents, and the government need to be considered, but they are basically subordinate to the child's best interests. This is the common thread that runs through the laws, with little variation, from state to state.

CHAPTER

2

Parties to an Adoption

Generally speaking, there are three primary parties to each adoption: the child, the prospective adoptive family, and the birth parent(s). These parties are not always "parties" to the case, as the term is used in the law, but they are the participants in the process.

The Child

No doubt, adoption is all about helping a child acquire a permanent family and a secure, stable upbringing. The child's interests are paramount, and everything that happens in the process feeds into this mandate. Upon completion of the adoption in court, the adoptee becomes the legal child of a new family which, going forward, has all rights, duties, and responsibilities for the child's welfare.

The benefits to the adoptee are many as he or she acquires a relatively permanent family (subject to the variety of issues, such as divorce, that would make such a family nonpermanent); relative emotional, social, and financial security; and the opportunity to develop emotional bonds with parents and, perhaps, siblings, that would not have existed had the child not been adopted. Every case will offer its own specific and unique variety of benefits to the child.

Public policy favors adoption of children whose parents' rights have been terminated – voluntarily or involuntarily – versus a child being an "orphan" or ward of the state. Since most adoptees are placed with families with adequate financial resources, the chances of an adoptee becoming homeless or subject to a state's foster or welfare programs are greatly diminished, and thus, society is benefitted by adoption socially and financially. Additionally, through adoption, the adoptee acquires varying levels of financial security because he or she becomes the legal child of the adoptive parents, and thus acquires rights of inheritance from and through the adoptive family. The adoptive family presumably adopted the child voluntarily, so everybody wins.

The Interests of the Child Are First

Most adoptions of newborns are accomplished through state-licensed adoption agencies or through attorneys who are members of their state's bar association. The primary responsibilities of an adoption agency or an adoption attorney are to protect the child, to act in the best interest of the child, and to take steps to provide the child with a safe, sound, secure, and stable living environment. They must also be zealous advocates for their clients' interests, of course, but never to the exclusion of the best interests of the child.

To fulfill this responsibility and thus to make an informed and intelligent placement of a child, the child's background information must be procured and evaluated before making a match of the child with a prospective adoptive family. What is in the best interest of the child will be dependent on the particular needs of the particular child, and the ability of a prospective adoptive family to meet those needs. In the world of adoption, there is no one-size-fits-all solution to anything, and thus each adoption must be the product of very specific and professional care, attention, planning, and execution.

But what if the child is unborn at the time the prospective adoptive family is matched with the birth parent(s) for the prospective adoption? In such cases – which make up the vast majority of adoptions through our agency – the only way to make a responsible decision regarding a placement is to gather as much background information about the birth parent(s) and the pregnancy as possible. Such information should include every variety of detail you can think of, including, but certainly not limited to, the birth parents' ethnicity, educational background, medical history (including family members), occupational history, legal history, family history, and, among others, legal issues (such as criminal background, if any). Various items of information will be available in any given case, sometimes more, sometimes less. The information collected by the attorney or agency about the birth parent(s) and their families should be shared and discussed, in its entirety and without exception, with the prospective adoptive family. That is to say, all of it must be shared: the good, the bad, and the ugly.

On the handful of occasions where our Agency has become involved in the placement of a child who is "older," and we have used our office as part of the gentle transition into the new family, we have taken advantage of the situation to provide additional information to the adoptive family. Specifically, when toddlers come to the office we love to offer them paper and crayons so they can draw and color. The product of their play/art sessions is always given to the adoptive family, just in case there is meaning to be found in the product.

Of particular importance to the prospective adoptive family is the birth parents' and their extended family's genetic and hereditary factors or pathology to the extent reasonably available. This information may shed light on a child's anticipated developmental capabilities and could permit early intervention in an area where the genetic or hereditary factors point to a specific challenge for the child after birth.

The Prospective Adoptive Family

The process of adoption enables a family – in many cases after years of frustration and anxiety over not being able to expand their family in the traditional biological way – to finally become parents. Adoption is obviously not the only method of family creation or expansion, but it is one that has become extremely practical and accepted to accomplish the goal of having a child or adding another child to a family when other efforts have been unsuccessful.

As discussed in more detail elsewhere in this text, the prospective adoptive family must undergo some pretty rigorous screenings in order to be approved by an agency, an attorney, and a court to adopt a baby. But the rewards can be immeasurable. Similar to the way that some women sometimes say that parenthood makes them forget the pain of childbirth, we often hear adoptive parents claim that the joys (and disappointments) of being parents through adoption often completely replace their recollection of many years of disappointment, frustration, and anxiety associated with their unsuccessful attempts to procreate biologically. In other words, many adoptive families have described their successful adoptions as the end to a long nightmare.

It is the prospective adoptive family who, upon being matched with the expectant birth parents, embarks on what can often be accurately described as a "roller coaster ride." The family is essentially placing their trust and confidence in the ability and willingness of the birth parent(s) to complete the stated adoption plan and to surrender the baby to the family, through the agency or the attorney, after the child's birth, and then to not interfere with the required legal process to finalize the adoption. Sometimes this works out beautifully. Other times it's much easier said than done.

The prospective adoptive family faces a number of risks in the adoption of a newborn, ranging from the motivations of the birth parent(s) to the health of the child at birth and later in life.

It is the prospective adoptive family which must undergo the home study process which involves, among other items, legal background checks (criminal as well as civil), medical examinations, personal reference letters from nonrelatives and production of employment and financial verification records. Further, the family is subject to extensive counseling on issues ranging from caring for a newborn to eventually having a discussion with the child (at an appropriate age) about the fact that he or she was adopted, the circumstances surrounding the birth parent(s), and the decision to place the child for adoption. Even further, the prospective adoptive parents may choose eventually to discuss the facts and circumstances surrounding the actual match and the events thereafter which lead to the finalization of the adoption.

It is also the prospective adoptive family which bears the almost incomprehensible financial and emotional risks associated with many adoptions of newborns. Those risks include, but are certainly not limited to, any undisclosed medical history of the birth parent(s), the possibility of a loss of the pregnancy or the child at birth, and the possibility that the birth parent(s) never intended to place the as-yet-unborn child for adoption and was basically scamming the prospective adoptive family out of money. Additional risks include the risk that regardless of how compliant the birth mother is with regard to her medical visits and following her doctor's instructions, the baby could be born with health issues which are undetectable at birth and are not known until years after birth. For example, a heart murmur is detectable at birth but autism is not. So, these, among many other risks, are part of the adoption process.

The Birth Parent(s)

It takes two to tango. Nonetheless, it is oftentimes only the birth mother who seeks adoption placement help for the unborn child, as the fathers all too often plant the seed but don't stick around for long thereafter. In the words of brilliant family law litigator Anthony Marchese, Esq., they "beget and begone." For that practical reason, we concentrate herein on our dealings with the birth mother, and raise matters relevant to the birth father wherever and whenever applicable.

(Since many of the adoptions we've handled have involved the participation of only the birth mother but not the birth father, we reference – sometimes parenthetically – the birth father, but focus on the birth mother. So when you read about obtaining information about the "birth parent(s)," we are really dialing in on the birth mother and suggesting that the birth father is often not a part of the actual adoption equation and very often the birth mother goes through the process without the participation of the birth father.)

To say the very least, hats off to the birth parents who make the difficult and selfless decision to provide a child, through adoption, with a better life than they are able to provide for the child at that particular time in their life. Depending on the specific circumstances, voluntarily placing a child for adoption can take an incredible amount of selflessness and commitment to doing what's best for the child, even though often painful for the birth parent(s). At other times, the decision, while voluntary, is practically made for the birth parent(s) by their specific living circumstances, health, legal issues, family circumstances, and other factors. Either way, it's not usually a decision that is made with overwhelming delight.

For the voluntarily consenting birth parent(s), the decision to place a child for adoption comes with both positives and negatives. The positives include absolution of the financial and emotional responsibilities of raising a child who may have been the result of an unplanned and/or unexpected pregnancy and the knowledge that the child's financial and emotional needs will be met by an adoptive family.

We are frequently told that the decision to place a child for adoption is a great relief to a birth parent who is desirous of doing what's in the best interests of the child and who knows that, at that point in her life, she is simply unable to reasonably provide the emotional and financial needs of the child. Further, for a birth parent who wants to continue his or her education or develop other skills which may help provide a more productive and rewarding future, the adoption removes a potential hindrance to such accomplishments while simultaneously providing the birth parent with inner peace in knowing that the child will be safe and secure in a stable family.

On the negative side, the decision to place a child for adoption can be emotionally painful to the birth parent and her family whether it be the child's siblings, cousins, grandparents, or other relatives. This negative impact results from either the selfless decision by the birth parent to place the child for adoption or from a decision practically made for her by "the system," which might include a state's child welfare department, guardian ad litem, or a judge. The choice of adoption may also be based on the decision of the birth parent that she simply does not want the responsibilities that are attached to a lifetime of parenthood. Whatever motivates the decision to place a child for adoption, it is a huge step in the direction of the child likely having a more stable and secure life.

One of the most important steps and the "center of gravity" in the overall adoption process is the identification of bona fide birth parents who are actually and genuinely seeking assistance in placing a child for adoption. Unless you've worked in an agency or for an adoption attorney, you can't begin to imagine the variety of incoming calls from people claiming to want to place a child for adoption ranging from the most bizarre to the most sincere to the most fraudulent and just about anything and everything in between.

Birth parent(s) have a variety of motivations for placing a child for adoption, ranging from the best interests of the child to their own lifestyle and life path choices. Rarely, is it an easy decision.

We were contacted by a woman named Jaclyn who was in her fourth month of pregnancy, carrying a girl, which was not surprising since she already had three of them. This struggling single mother of three girls was yet again pregnant, yet again unexpectedly, but this time realized that she just couldn't keep and raise another child.

There are two remarkable stories within this story: (1) The birth father issue and (2) the surprise decision made by Jaclyn at the end of the case.

This story starts when we were subject to a law, which lasted from 2001 to 2003, under which birth mothers were responsible for finding and notifying any and all prospective biological fathers – even rapists – that they were placing a baby for adoption.

In real life it wasn't the birth mothers at all to whom that burden fell. It was, of course, the adoption professionals who were ultimately charged with

continued

continued

finding and notifying putative fathers, many of whom wanted nothing to do with any baby or mother.

Jaclyn was a well-spoken, energetic, and friendly young lady with bright red hair. She did not drink or do drugs, had a better-than-average education, and loved to read. When I met her in her home she was well-dressed (by which I mean she was dressed better than I was), greeted me warmly, and invited me in and introduced me to her three beautiful daughters. Her clean and tidy small home was adorned with pictures of her girls at various church and school events. Jaclyn was friendly, all smiles, and spoke in that semi-southern way some people do, with "god damns" replaced by "gosh darns," etc. You know the type.

Surprisingly to me, and seemingly inconsistent with her character as I had judged it in the brief encounter, Jaclyn claimed to have no idea as to the identity of the father of the pregnancy. Without going into all the details, Jaclyn ultimately disclosed that the birth father could be one of a dozen or so males.

Some have asked me why I didn't call DCF to report this behavior, considering the fact that this woman was the mother and caretaker of three young girls.

continued

Sadly, there are scammers who look to take advantage of prospective adopters. To avoid scammers, it's best to work through an adoption agency or experienced attorney.

CAUTION

The most common calls are from women who have an unplanned pregnancy, claim to have no present intent or desire to parent the child and who do not want to terminate their pregnancy either because they are opposed to abortion or because they would like to have the baby placed in a loving home with the likelihood of a more stable life than they are able to provide at that particular time in their life. In so doing, they also recognize that they will be making a family's dream come true while simultaneously giving the child an opportunity at a life otherwise unavailable.

There are also calls from women who recognize that they have no maternal instincts or skills and don't want to consider raising a child, women who simply want to place the baby for adoption knowing that their reasonable and necessary living expenses and medical bills will be paid for by an adoptive family (in states where permitted), and women who call with absolutely no intent to place a baby for adoption (and sometimes are not even pregnant) and are looking to scam some unsuspecting and vulnerable family seeking to adopt a child. Scammers most often try to identify prospective adoptive families via the Internet or through offbeat publications or personal contacts as opposed to through the services of an experienced and savvy private agency or attorney. The reason for this is that, in many (but certainly not all) cases, the scam would be fairly obvious to an adoption professional and may not be as obvious to a vulnerable family without experienced representation. More on scams later.

Sometimes the birth mother calls with the present intention of placing a child for adoption, but with requirements for the case that are so outrageous and untenable that we simply would never put a client in the situation she's proposing. For example, from time to time we'll receive a call from a woman claiming to want to place her as-yet-unborn child for adoption, but requiring as part of the adoption agreement that the adoptive parents essentially become little more than nannies and housekeepers. Specifically, the birth mother will say she wants to place the baby for adoption with a family chosen by her, and that the family must agree to allow the birth mother to have what amounts to unfettered access to and decision-making over the raising of the child. The birth mother wants to attend all parties, graduations, etc. She wants to tell them what church to go to, how to educate, and where to school the child. She wants unlimited access to time with the child including, but not limited to, sleepovers, either at her residence or that of the child.

NO. Not happening. There are postadoption communication and/or contact arrangements that are beneficial, but arranging for babysitting and calling it adoption is not in the best interest of anyone.

The process of identifying birth parents typically starts with a woman calling the agency or the adoption attorney. In the first telephone call, a skilled and experienced agency representative or attorney should be able to pick up certain words, expressions, and phrases which may be a tip-off that the caller is trying to convince the agency or attorney of her bona fide

continued

Her lifestyle choice is not illegal, and there is no reason to believe, based on my interview with her, that her children were in any way at risk of any type of abuse and/or neglect. In fact, at the time of this interview I was sitting with Jaclyn in her clean home watching her clean, well-mannered, and healthy-looking children play!

She delivered this information as if it was something "normal" or to be expected. There was not a bit of shame in her delivery, mannerism, or facial expression. Hard as it was to keep a straight face, I soldiered on with the interview, gathering all of the necessary family, health, and other miscellaneous information which I would need to move forward with Jaclyn's adoption plan. Toward the end of the conversation I wondered to myself whether I had only imagined that first part!

Suffice it to say, I did my due diligence in attempting to locate the birth father based on the information Jaclyn provided. Not surprisingly, no one stepped forward.

Sometime around the sixth month of pregnancy, Jaclyn decided she missed the party life, which was preferable to the working-mom life that she had created for herself via her three girls, all of whom were unexpected. Jaclyn had met the couple, Tom and Diane, who was on deck to adopt the baby in a few months, and liked them. Clearly.

Jaclyn called me with an idea she had, and presented it as if it was an unimportant passing thought. She was wondering whether, and thought it would be a great idea if, Tom and Diane would be willing to adopt *all three of her girls*, followed by the newborn! I was absolutely shocked, as none of us saw this coming.

continued

The reality is that most birth parents(s) are in some type of distress. Some may have substance abuse or other issues. Prospective adopters need to be both wary and understanding of the birth mother situation.

NOTE

continued

Tom and Diane were a couple in their mid-30s expecting their first child via this adoption. They had no experience in raising babies let alone children! I could not imagine that this would be part of their plan. Wrong I was. They jumped *through the phone* and somehow were in my office faster than I thought was possible, filling out forms and starting that process! The social worker who wrote their home study was contacted and once again to my surprise was very excited for them, thinking they would be great parents for this unusual situation, despite their relative lack of experience. A plan was put in place to give them the support and supervision they needed should this multiple sibling group adoption actually go through.

The three girls, aged 8, 6, and 2, had three different fathers, only one of whom was known and identifiable. (You would have thought that these girls had no paternal input whatsoever, as the three of them were essentially clones of their mother, who obviously carried with her some very strong DNA! There was enough beautiful red hair in that family to keep a touring production of Annie on the road for a decade.) The sole identifiable birth father, father of the middle child, was more than delighted to hear that

continued

intent to place the baby for adoption (or not). For this reason we NEVER use an answering service. There is an actual representative of or attorney for the agency on call 24/7/365, answering calls as they come in. Is that horrible for the person on call, who has to keep his phone within arm's reach 24/7, and has to walk out the door of movies and concerts to field calls at all hours, godly and otherwise? Yes. Is it crucial for serving the needs of the agency's clients. Well, it's close enough to crucial to necessitate doing it.

If our initial impression is that the prospective birth mother on the phone is sincere and isn't covered head to toe in red flags, we will arrange to meet with her as soon as we reasonably can, depending upon schedules and location. If possible and with her permission, we will run a cursory investigation on her, including a computer background check, prior to meeting with her. Same goes for the birth father, if applicable. We will also enter her name into a search engine to see what other information, if any, is available in the public domain, and every effort will be made to verify the parts of her story we were able to ascertain from the initial phone call. In short, we want to know with whom we're meeting, and we want to know the answers to our questions about her background even before we ask them.

On the subject of "red flags," it's important to note that the life and lifestyle of some of the women who call for adoption assistance is nontraditional, to say the least. People who are looking for help in placing a baby for adoption are almost always in some type of distress. If a woman calls and admits within the first few minutes of a telephone call that she's in distress, on the streets, addicted to drugs, prostituting for drug money, being beaten by a pimp, pregnant by an unknown party, unsure of how far along she is, in need of immediate help with funds for food and/or shelter, or any combination of these factors, it's probably true. Believe it or not, these are not "red flags." This is not atypical of the population served by the adoption professionals of the world. Much like a police officer or firefighter will run *toward* a disaster while others are running away, this type of caller, if sincere about her plan, is carrying a baby who desperately needs us to run in its direction and help it find a more stable life situation.

continued

he would be able to stop paying child support for the child he had never seen and in whom he had no interest. He eagerly consented to the adoption.

In the long run, Tom and Diane adopted all four girls, all of whom looked exactly like Jaclyn!

Who May Adopt

The world of adoption, like the world in general, continues to evolve right before our eyes. Decades ago, adoptions were almost entirely pursued by the so-called "traditional" heterosexual married couple where the adoptive mother was the stay-at-home mom and the adoptive father was the breadwinner. The old-fashioned "traditional" is no longer the norm in our adoption practice, and we know that to be the case in many other agencies and adoption attorney's offices as well.

Single-Parent Adoptions

In the past, so-called "traditional" adoptions were mostly pursued by infertile heterosexual married couples. When a single person wanted to adopt a child, an eyebrow might have been raised, especially if that person was a male. Nowadays it is not uncommon nor is it thought of as unusual for single men and single women to want to adopt nor is it uncommon for them to be chosen by birth parents to adopt their children. In fact, many birth mothers are especially attracted to the situation of single parents or same-sex couples, who wouldn't be able to have children were it not for one of these alternative methods of family creation.

The law clearly recognizes that single people are eligible to adopt and birth parents are oftentimes understanding of a single person's desire to realize the joys of parenthood without a spouse. As long as a single parent's circumstances provide the child with the opportunity for a safe, sound, stable, and secure life, the law permits and societal norms accept single parents to adopt.

Ultimately, the birth parent(s) can decide who adopts her or their child, subject to court approval. While some may be open to single-parent adoptions, others may not.

It goes without saying, but we'll say it anyway, that the decision to place the child with a single parent (or any parent for that matter) must be made with the child's best interests at the forefront of the decision-making process. That said, the birth parents do have the right to insist on a "traditional" prospective adoptive family and there are some adoption agencies and attorneys which will tacitly (or sometimes overtly) discourage placement of a child with a single parent regardless of the fact that the state law permits single-parent adoptions. Ultimately, however, in most cases and subject to court approval, the birth parent has the final word on who adopts her child.

Consider the birth parent who was raised by a single parent and who is unhappy about being deprived of, in most cases and among other things, a present father. Those birth parents may insist on (or at least have a strong preference for) a married couple to adopt the child to avoid the child having similar feelings or being raised in a similar fashion. On the other hand, a birth parent who was raised by a single parent, or who is herself a single parent, may very well see no reason to deny another single parent the experience of parenting. So, as you can see, it is a personal preference for the birth parents and it is up to them to choose the composition of the family, again subject to court approval.

Birth parents, licensed agencies, and adoption attorneys have multiple and oftentimes differing goals, and a successful adoption requires choreographing and reconciling those goals such that at the end of the day the birth parent knows that her child will be well cared for, the adoptive family experiences the thrill of parenthood, and, of course, the child becomes a legal member of a loving family.

Stepparent Adoptions

The stepparent adoption is the most common of the relative adoptions. The typical form of stepparent adoption involves a man who is married to a child's biological mother and wishes to adopt her child. The child usually lives with the biological mother and her new husband and has had recent contact with his or her birth father who is typically the noncustodial parent. If it's the mother's new husband seeking to adopt the child and the identity of the birth father is known, bitter disputes can arise between the custodial parent (the mother), her husband, and the noncustodial birth father. If there is a problem, it typically surrounds the birth father's unwillingness to consent to the adoption of the child by the birth mother's new husband fearing that he (the birth father) will lose contact with the child.

As a general proposition, it is necessary to obtain the consent of the parent whose rights are going to be terminated by the stepparent adoption. That parent's cooperation, when necessary, will determine whether the proposed stepparent adoption will be a walk in the park or a nuclear war.

For example, if the birth father does not consent to the adoption by the birth mother's new spouse, terminating the parental rights of the birth father can become a legal struggle and a determination must be made as to whether the birth father's rights can be terminated involuntarily based on his conduct during the child's life or other factors. In the absence of a voluntary consent, a parent's rights are generally terminable based on abuse, neglect, or abandonment of the child by the parent, and an experienced lawyer in any given jurisdiction would be able to give an educated guess as to the difficulty of accomplishing an involuntary termination in any given case. As in all adoptions, the question of what's in the best interest of the child will play a paramount role in a stepparent adoption.

Other factors which may interfere with or facilitate the accomplishment of a stepparent adoption include issues such as where, geographically, the new family will live; how the child(ren) will treat or refer to the stepparent versus the biological parent; and, of course, the issue of whether the terminated parent will have to pay any back or future child support.

Sarah and Lorenzo are the biological parents of three-year-old Li'l Treyvon. Sarah is the custodial parent, and Lorenzo is $6,000 behind on child support. Sarah meets Jennifer, they date and fall in love. Sarah and Jennifer marry, and Jennifer wants to adopt Li'l Treyvon in a stepparent adoption. They approach Lorenzo to ask him if he'll consent, and he replies, predictably, that he'll consent, but only if Sarah agrees to waive the back child support. (Lorenzo already knows that the adoption will absolve him of any *future* child support.)

Who has a right to the back child support, Sarah or Li'l Treyvon? If Lorenzo gives his consent in exchange for the elimination of his $6,000 debt, isn't that tantamount to him "selling" his consent? "Baby selling," or the exchange of money for adoption, is illegal in any US jurisdiction I can think of. How that should be handled in the case of a stepparent adoption? The answers to these legal and public policy issues are for the legislatures and courts to decide, but it becomes conceptually problematic to either allow such behavior, thus legalizing a form of baby selling, or to prohibit such behavior, thus taking away the opportunity for the Li'l Treyvons of the world to have a two-parent family.

In a garden-variety, uncontested stepparent adoption, for example, the husband of the mother who gave birth to the child while she was not married to the father of the child, legislatures have been quick to streamline the rules of procedure which would otherwise require a home study, extensive FBI, local law enforcement, child abuse, and other background checks. The result of the law's streamlining of often unnecessary, time-consuming, and costly steps is that the family which is already conducting themselves as a legal family will be recognized in the eyes of the law and by all others as a legal family. Thus, the law often recognizes that some of the procedures which are wholly appropriate in private adoptions serve no purpose in stepparent adoptions.

If appropriate based on the child's age and intellectual capacity, it is important to discuss the proposed stepparent adoption with the child and to understand the child's feelings toward the adoption. Your state's law will be the determining factor as to whether the child's consent is required to complete the stepparent adoption. Parents of teens who are hoping to do this ought to be nice to their kids, as the kids may have veto power over your family's legal plans! This is one of the many areas in which law and social work intersect. Every case is different, and every child has his or her unique needs and rights.

Again, if appropriate based on the child's age and intellectual capacity, the child should be consulted with or at least informed as to any name change which may result from the adoption and be given the opportunity to express an opinion as to whether the last name given at birth or a new last name after the adoption is preferable. The idea, of course, is to make the stepparent adoption a harmonious and positive step in the life of the family as a whole, but especially for the child.

When the process is complete, the stepparent becomes the legal parent of the child for all purposes. As the new legal parent of the child, the stepparent acquires, by law, the rights, duties, responsibilities, and obligations that would exist if he or she was the child's biological parent.

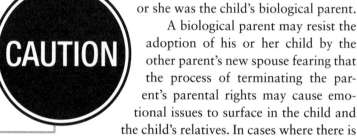

In a stepparent adoption (as with all adoptions), the child's interest is paramount. If a teenage child objects to stepparent adoption, it very well may sway the court to reject the adoption.

A biological parent may resist the adoption of his or her child by the other parent's new spouse fearing that the process of terminating the parent's parental rights may cause emotional issues to surface in the child and the child's relatives. In cases where there is any uncertainty as to the effects of a stepparent adoption, the parties should seek counseling through their adoption agency or other resources. Parents need to remember that the child is the party with the most needs and least resources, and the parents' selfish desires to accomplish their goals, whatever they may be, ought to be subordinate to what's best legally, psychologically, socially, and emotionally for the child.

Procedurally, a petition for stepparent adoption must be filed with all exhibits required by state law (i.e., consent of birth mother, consent of birth father, if available, and consent of the child if required by state law). If all required consents are received, the next step is setting up a final hearing at which time the judge may make some inquiry into issues he or she believes are important to know in order to act in a manner deemed to be in the child's best interests. Once satisfied that the stepparent adoption is in the child's best interests, a final judgment of adoption is signed by the judge and an application for a new birth certificate is filed identifying the legal parents of the child and showing the new name, if applicable, of the child. The noncustodial parent's parental rights are terminated in this procedure.

Adoptions by "Homosexuals"

There has been a sea change recently in the manner in which gay and lesbian families are treated legally and socially, including as it relates to state adoption laws. Historically, birth parents, adoption agencies, and adoption attorneys would favor the so-called "traditional" family, with a husband and a wife. Then, a heterosexual single-parent adoption enjoyed wider acceptance. Now, times have certainly changed. In fact, until 2011, Florida was the only state in the United States with an outright prohibition against adoption by a " homosexual." It took until 2011 for various courts of appeal to rule that such a prohibition is unconstitutional and now "homosexuals" are permitted to adopt in Florida.

I wrote a guest column for the *South Florida Gay News* prior to the lifting of the prohibition of "homosexuals" from adopting. It's included in the appendix. It's important to note that the legal and constitutional reasoning for the overturning of the ban was *not* the reasoning outlined in this column, but we stand by it as solid and logical reasoning nonetheless.

The subject of the availability of adoptions for same-sex couples (married or not), and gay or lesbian singles, is definitely one which comes with much controversy and with opposing viewpoints. While the main concern should be the good and welfare of the child, the propriety of such adoptions is a cause for debate along social, familial, religious, and political lines. It is a topic on which there will always be disagreement.

NOTE

With the change in laws and societal attitudes, birth parent(s) increasingly are accepting of same-sex couple adoptions. As a result, same-sex couple adoptions are almost commonplace.

Various studies have either supported or opposed adoption by same-sex couples, proving scientifically without a shadow of a doubt that (a) parents' sexual orientation in and of itself does not adversely affect the normal social and emotional development of a child or (b) children raised by gay or lesbian parents suffer some type of social and/or emotional deficit, and therefore, gays and lesbians should be prohibited from adopting. (In case you were unaware, the commissioner of a study can pay to have the result they're hoping for.)

So far as we can tell, the actual independent research and general consensus suggests that children who are adopted, nurtured, and raised by gay and lesbian singles or couples are on at least equal footing socially, emotionally, and intellectually with children raised by heterosexual couples or singles. And so, there has been a noticeable and more frequent acceptance of gay and lesbian couples and singles selected by birth parents to adopt their children. It remains, however, within a judge's discretion to determine whether a particular adoption is in the child's best interests. The point here is that a court decision cannot be made solely on the basis of sexual orientation. If the gay or lesbian person or the same-sex couple otherwise meets the state's requirements, the adoption should proceed.

That said and subject to the approval of the court, the adoption agency, and the adoption attorney, the ultimate decision as to whether any person or couple may adopt lies in the hands of the birth parent(s) in the typical private adoption scenario wherein the birth parents are involved to some extent in the selection of the adoptive family.

Our experience in this field suggests that the possibilities for same-sex couples to adopt have advanced rapidly and it is no longer an uncommon sight to see a same-sex couple in court for a final hearing of adoption. In fact, to facilitate these adoptions and for accuracy and fairness, some states have even changed their birth certificate application procedures to provide for "Parent 1" and "Parent 2" applications, as opposed to the conventional and more traditional "Husband" and "Wife" or "Father" and "Mother" applications. Thus, when the new birth certificate is issued after the adoption is finalized, the same-sex parents are identified as "Parent 1" and "Parent 2."

As with most aspects of adoption, the availability of a child for adoption by a so-called "nontraditional" family is almost entirely dependent on the agreement to place the child with the same-sex family by the birth parent(s), subject, as above, to judicial, agency, or attorney approval, which approval cannot be unreasonably withheld for discriminatory purposes. Our experience as adoption professionals is that more and more birth parents are accepting of, and are placing children with, same-sex couples, and we see no indication that this will change anytime soon.

Relative Adoptions

It seems that the number of grandparent and relative adoptions trends upward along with the rates of unemployment and drug and alcohol abuse by young parents. This particular type of adoption is very much influenced by general economic factors which might cause parents to be financially unable to provide for their children but unwilling to place the children for adoption with anyone other than a relative.

In raising a relative's child, there are many important concerns which need to be considered, discussed, agreed upon, and implemented. Like every other adoption, the goal of this type of adoption is to put the child in a situation wherein the parents responsible for raising the child are most concerned with the physical and emotional well-being of the child, as opposed to what benefit(s) they can personally derive from whatever assistance comes with the adoptive placement.

One issue which birth parents sometimes have a hard time swallowing is the fact that the new adoptive parents, who are, in some cases, the birth parent's own parents (thus the child's biological grandparents) are now the individuals who have the rights and responsibilities to make decisions for the child and to raise the child in the way that they see fit. In many cases, interference by the biological parents is unwelcome.

To put it bluntly, it was the acts and/or omissions of the birth parent(s) that necessitated the transfer of parental rights in the first place, so there's no reason to believe that continuation of that person's parental style would be suddenly be appropriate or in the best interest of the child. Therefore, the relative adoption keeps the child in the family and gives him or her another shot at getting decent parenting.

To sum it up, if the child is adopted by a relative, there is no extra or additional restriction imposed upon the relative's right to make all decisions for the child, as that relative becomes the child's legal parent.

Guardianship

The circumstances under which the relatives become custodians or guardians of the child will affect the relatives' adoption. If the child was removed from the biological parents by a state child protective agency because the birth parent(s) abused, neglected, or abandoned the child and are deemed to be unfit, the relative–child relationship will likely be supervised to some extent by the state until the time a legal adoption is completed. In this situation, the relative's legal rights to secure services for the child may be the subject of a court order delineating what decisions for health care and educational and other services the relative may make. It will not, however, make the child the legal child of the relative, and thus, it will not give the relative complete rights to make decisions for and on behalf of the child as if the relative was the biological parent of the child.

If the birth parent(s) chooses to have a child live with and be raised by a relative, an out-of-court arrangement may be made through, for example, a power of attorney or voluntary guardianship which would give the relative authority to make specific enumerated decisions on behalf of the child. It should be noted that while this approach does give the relative specific authority to do certain things for the child, it can generally be revoked by the birth parent(s) under certain pre–agreed-upon circumstances.

If the goal of the birth parent(s) is to have a relative adopt the child, the adoption process would result in the permanent termination of parental rights of the birth parents and the establishment of the relative as the legal parent of the child with all legal, moral, and ethical rights, duties, and obligations of any parent. The significance of the relative adoption is that it gives the child a sense of belonging and stability which the birth parent is presumably unable to provide at that juncture in time, and it keeps the child in the family to which he or she has a biological connection.

Aunts, uncles, brothers, sisters, cousins, and other relatives are permitted to adopt children subject to the laws of the state in which the proceeding is to take place. Certain relatives are excluded from the group of people who require FBI and local law enforcement clearances or child-abuse clearances and will not have to have a home study. The exclusion of a relative from these requirements is based on that relative's closeness in lineal heritage to the child. To determine whether these reports and studies are necessary, it is important to ascertain the degree of connection between the adoptee and the new prospective adoptive parent through a "table of consanguinity." There is variation from table to table, so it is important to find the system used by the court in your jurisdiction.

There may be other legal requirements from which relatives are exempt and which will make the relative adoption process more efficient, less time-consuming,

TIP

Assuming the birth parent is willing, adoption by a family member provides for a less burdensome and more efficient adoption process than adoption by a nonfamily member.

and less costly. It is important to check the applicable state laws to determine what is and what is not required to complete a relative adoption.

Foster Family Adoptions

Let's start with the difference between adoption and foster care. Adoption is a permanent change in the legal status and life of a child and involves a lifetime commitment to the child on a legal, ethical, and emotional level. The adoptive family has the unequivocal legal right to decide on the issues of, among many others, health care, education, travel as well as future contacts, if any, with the child's biological parent(s). The right and responsibility to make those decisions is vested in the adoptive parents until the child is 18 years of age at which point the child can generally make his or her own decisions as an adult.

Foster care, on the other hand, is a temporary arrangement and typically involves a child who has been removed from the biological parent(s) due to some form of abuse, neglect, abandonment, or some other situation which would deem the parent(s) unfit or which would deem it inappropriate and not in the child's best interests to remain in the care and custody of the birth parent(s). In such cases, the child is often placed temporarily with another family until the decision as to the permanent placement of the child or reunification with the birth parent(s) is made. That decision could be either placing the child with a responsible family member who has passed the aforementioned numerous regulatory hurdles, reunification of the child with the birth parent(s) at such time as they "have their act together," or the termination of parental rights enabling a qualified family not known to the birth parent(s) to adopt the child. Sometimes, a child who was in a temporary foster placement pending the outcome of the birth parent(s) case plan will ultimately permanently adopt the child.

While foster parents have limited legal parental rights to the child, upon completion of an adoption (if they are ultimately able and willing to adopt the child), they acquire full legal rights to the child as if the child was born to them, and the child transitions from being in the state's legal custody to being a full-fledged member of the adoptive (former foster) family.

Foster care usually begins with the removal of a child from his situation and placement of that child in emergency shelter care, followed by a court-ordered reunification plan in which the state promotes the idea and hope that the child can and will be reunified with one or both birth parents once the situation causing the removal of the child by the state's child welfare agency is remedied and the court deems the birth parent(s) fit to regain custody of the child. The successful completion of the reunification plan is often based on the birth parent(s) substantially completing an arduous and often very demanding list of tasks to demonstrate fitness to resume their parental roles with respect to the child. While the tasks that comprise the plan are often comprehensive, the birth parent(s) is often given a great deal of leeway and wiggle room in their completion.

All too often, the birth parents are unwilling or unable to comply with the state's requirements and tasks deemed necessary to regain custody of the child. When their efforts fail, they are usually given additional chances to succeed. If and at such time the birth parent(s) run out of chances, such failure may open the door to the foster family being offered the opportunity to adopt the child and give the child a permanent family. This would be considered to be a change in the case plan "goal" from reunification to termination of parental rights.

Depending on a child's age, it often happens that a child is moved from one foster home to another one or more times making it difficult for the child to feel attached to any one family. A child may feel secure with a particular foster family while simultaneously having feelings of affection or love for his or her biological family despite whatever incident(s) occurred to necessitate the removal of the child from the birth parent(s). This can cause conflicting feelings and emotions for the child when the parental rights of the biological parents are terminated and the child is moving toward permanency through adoption by a foster family. This emotion is likely to be directly influenced by whether or not the birth parent(s) consider adoption

Here's something interesting: Florida's ban on "homosexuals" adopting children came off the books in June of 2015, but was declared unconstitutional and therefore unenforceable a few years prior. However, Florida had no such ban on "homosexuals" *fostering* children. In a series of nationally publicized cases, gay foster parents were given the responsibility to foster children in the system, oftentimes the children were HIV positive. In some cases, after years and years had passed and those children were firmly entrenched in and members of what was, in many cases, the only family they ever knew, the children became available for permanent adoption. Due to the legal ban, those families were told that the children were being removed from their homes for placement with total strangers. The notion embedded in Florida law at the time that living temporarily with "homosexuals" was ok, but permanent adoption by them was illegal was clearly absurd. The sad result was that children, in many cases, were ripped out of their family and given, at a very sensitive time in their development, to total strangers.

by a foster family to be in the best interest of the child. No doubt, it's a difficult spot for most children to be in as their skills have not developed to the point where they can understand the dynamics behind the decisions that must be made by any combination of biological parents, the state, the court, and the foster family. Once again, social work and counseling can go a long way toward making this situation more acceptable for the child as well as the birth parent(s).

Depending upon the specific terms of the adoption, it may also enable the child to have some form of contact with the birth parents. This is entirely up to the adoptive family and the birth parent(s).

A foster family is always confronted with the risk that all of the time, energy, love, and affection they put into fostering a child may disappear in the blink of an eye. Their commitment to the child's development, their efforts to integrate the child into their family, and everything else they did to prepare for the day when they would be able to adopt the child can crumble without warning. Such is the risk of fostering to adopt, but the rewards are immeasurable. Knowing how a child's life has been changed for the better is an awesome feeling and one which will be difficult to compare or duplicate.

A child in foster care may still have feelings of affection toward his birth family, despite what may have happened to cause his or her removal from the household. Foster parents looking to adopt need to be aware of the complexity of the emotions of such a child. The positive effects of a foster adoption can be significant. A foster adoption provides the child with (a) a permanent, forever family; (b) the security of knowing that there will be no more bouncing from one home to another; and (c) the opportunity to grow and develop relationships with others (parents, relatives, and siblings) and to build self-esteem. There may also be a financial component to the adoption wherein some type of recurring subsidy or compensation is provided to the adoptive family for the child's welfare, including availability, in some instances, of funds for higher education.

CAUTION

There are several financial incentives that accompany the adoption of a child in foster care. For example, adoptions of children in foster care are typically far less costly than conventional private newborn adoptions, especially where it comes to legal and other professional fees. Often those are picked up by the state. Further, while fostering, the family is often paid a monthly cash stipend by the state to defray the cost of caring for the child. While some of the financial incentives stop upon the child's adoption, there is a continuation of certain benefits (e.g., Medicaid, which eliminates the need for the foster family to pay any medical bills for the child). Further there are subsidies which may be available for the child's normal living expenses and there are financial benefits to assist the foster family in paying for legal fees of an adoption. Additionally, there may be educational benefits including a prepaid college tuition program or a vocational school program available to the family for the child. That said, clearly no one would or should choose to foster or adopt a child based on financial motives. The adoption of a child from foster care should be done solely out of love for and a desire to nurture a permanent relationship between the adoptive family and the child.

All children are deserving of a sound, stable, secure, loving, and permanent family. Whether that happens through biology or through adoption of a foster or non-foster child is irrelevant. The plain and simple fact is that all children are entitled to have a permanent family and foster adoptions are one of the many ways to achieve that goal.

Who Can Be Adopted

Our experience indicates that the most frequent adoptions are either stepchildren or newborn infants. But there are other types of adoptions worth noting.

If birth parents determine that they are either unwilling or unable to care for a child of any age, they can voluntarily place the child for adoption. Similarly, at least in Florida, even after a child has been removed from the birth parent(s) and placed in foster care, the child can be placed for adoption through a private agency which intervenes in the case as long as the placement of the child occurs prior to the termination of parental rights of the birth parents by the court.

"Older" children may be adopted, but the older the child, the more difficult it is to find a match for that child. There is a perception that older children carry a greater possibility of attachment issues, bonding issues, and, perhaps, behavioral problems. Abandonment and/or neglect is typically the reason that an "older" child becomes available for adoption in the first place, and the thought that irreparable harm has been done to a child is very scary to some prospective parents. This is not to say that these children should not be adopted; just the opposite is true. These children are likely to be very much in need of a stable family and may well react positively to a change of environment and to the security of knowing that they now have a forever family. But that, like most issues and adoption, depends on the circumstances of each case, and professional supervision of the family is absolutely crucial.

"Drop-In" Adoptions

Many agency and attorney adoptions involve newborn children and involve a birth mother interested in assuring the child a better life than she is then able to provide. The agency or attorney typically works with the birth mother for many months leading up to the delivery and placement of the baby for adoption, thus enabling the agency, the attorney, and the prospective adoptive family to have at least some medical and family history of the birth parent(s).

There are occasional situations where the birth mother of the child does not make an adoption plan in advance of the delivery of the baby and realizes at the time of birth that she is unwilling, unable, unprepared,

Here's an interesting situation concerning who can be adopted: In many states there is no age limit on people who can be adopted. This ranges from the understandable case of parents of a child of any age who simply cannot properly care for the child (or who are unwilling to do so) and decide that they would rather adopt the child, to the more peculiar real-life case of a 70-year-old man with no relatives on the planet and who was orphaned as a young child. This elderly man was adopted by someone who simply wanted him to have a legal family even at a late stage of his life. When confronted with this exact case, one might assume it to be an adoption motivated by some form of profit or financial incentive with the theory being that the 70-year-old man might have a valuable estate and the family adopting him may have the estate in their sites. After reviewing the facts with the elderly man and the family that wanted to adopt him, we concluded that it was not an adoption based on the expectation of financial gain in any way; rather, it was simply a genuine gesture of human kindness by one person to another. While the court was certainly surprised by a 70-year-old adoptee as contrasted with the typical less-than-1-year-old adoptee, nothing in the law prevented the adoption from being finalized resulting in the elderly man being adopted by the new family, a family which, until this late stage in his life, he never had.

And here's another amazing but true story about who can be adopted:

> Many years ago, prior to the pain pill epidemic and prior to the current quality of medical technology that can practically tell you the baby's name via ultrasound, we were working on an adoption

continued

continued

for a lovely professional family. The birth mother didn't smoke, drink, or use drugs and was very compliant in making all doctor appointments. The birth mother was expecting and did indeed deliver twins (a boy and a girl), and the prospective adoptive family could not have been happier.

Their happiness crashed when, at five days of age, the baby boy developed excessive bleeding in the bowel area. It came on very quickly, and there was nothing they could do for him. The baby boy died within days. Needless to say, the family was devastated by the loss but conflicted by their excitement about their new life as parents of the surviving twin and their responsibilities in this tragedy. It was a bittersweet moment if there ever was one. Our office participated in the funeral and the baby naming events. It is impossible to know which emotion overrode the other: the sadness of the death or the promise of a new life.

We explained to the family that unless something extraordinary took place, the surviving little girl would not be the legal sister of her biological brother. The twins' birth mother was still his legal mother because her rights had not yet been terminated in court. Once the adoption was finalized, the girl's legal parents would be the parents who adopted her. Thus, the two would no longer be related had we not taken some extraordinary measures.

The adoptive family wanted to demonstrate to the surviving twin the commitment they had to both her and her brother, and to provide the deceased child with a Jewish funeral, which was important to them. In order for that to happen, they would have to do something for which there was no

or otherwise not interested in parenting the baby and thus she places the baby for adoption very shortly after birth and without ever having made a plan prior to delivery. We respectfully refer to these situations as "drop-ins" due to the absence of any prior contact with the birth mother.

The fact patterns behind "drop-in" adoptions are fairly similar. One scenario occurs when the birth mother was living in a kind of "denial" of her pregnancy, thinking that she would awaken one day and the pregnancy would be gone. Or realizing she was pregnant, when faced with the reality of an actual live baby she just delivered who will be depending on her for everything, the birth mother realizes that she is either unwilling or unable emotionally and/or financially to parent the child. When faced with such a reality, women in these situations usually turn to their family, an adoption agency, or an adoption attorney to place the child for adoption.

For prospective adoptive families, there are advantages as well as disadvantages to a drop-in adoption scenario.

The advantages to the adoption professionals and to the prospective adoptive families include the following:

- The baby is born, and it is known, at least preliminarily, what, if any, initial health issues exist. It is common for a birth mother in this scenario to have skipped the usual regimen of prenatal care, and thus, there is no medical testing, ultrasound, or other screening information on which to base a family's decision to proceed with an adoption.

continued

continued

• The anxiety and uncertainty of the waiting period during which a prospective adoptive family has to agonize over whether the birth mother will complete her adoption plan or refuse to consent to the adoption is eliminated. She's either going to place or she's not. In states wherein there is no "revocation waiting period," the birth mother's execution of the adoption consent and related paperwork pretty much puts an end to the wondering, without having to have lived with the anxiety for all those months.

• Because the birth mother was not being financially supported by the agency or adoption attorney, the cost of the adoption may well be lower than the usual adoption.

In many "drop-in" adoption cases there is an unknown or " refuse to identify" birth father requiring the agency or attorney to either search the state's putative (presumed) father registry, if there is one, or to otherwise comply with other legal requirements to assure that the unknown birth father has received his constitutional due process via legal notice published in a newspaper of the fact that the child he created is being placed for adoption.

In many cases we've dealt with, the birth mother chooses not to meet the prospective adoptive family with her main focus being on recovering from the delivery, closing that chapter of her life, and moving forward.

The financial risk of the proposed adoption to the prospective adoptive family is very likely to be minimal because the birth mother has not been supported financially by the agency or attorney throughout the pregnancy. She may require

provision in Florida statutes, adopt the deceased baby. The birth mother was 100% on board with this plan.

When we filed the petition for termination of parental rights, we asked the court to terminate the parental rights of the birth mother as to both children (even though only one survived), and when we filed the petition for adoption, we asked the court to permit the family to adopt both of the children. The judge wisely disregarded the fact that there was no provision in the statutes for this type of action, and realized that the societal and familial value of letting it happen far outweighed any opposition, of which there was none.

And so it was that the family did, in fact, adopt the living as well as the deceased child in a most unusual court proceeding but one which the presiding judge mentioned was as moving and heartfelt a gesture by the family as one could imagine. The family could then know that the child over whom their family was mourning was their legal child and the legal brother of their daughter.

NOTE

While there can be complications, our experience with "drop-in" adoptions as adoption attorneys has been very positive. Usually, the birth mother simply wants to move on with her life and is happy that the baby is placed with a suitable family.

assistance as allowed by state law for postbirth recovery expenses, but by the time such expenses are paid, the consent papers have most likely been signed and the main risk that she will not complete her adoption plan is greatly reduced or eliminated.

There are also disadvantages of the "drop-in" adoption scenario. They are

- little or no confirmable knowledge of the birth mother's whereabouts or lifestyle during the pregnancy, including substance abuse or other actions which might have a direct impact on the health of the baby is available;
- prenatal records to ascertain possible medical or genetic issues confronting the baby are often nonexistent;
- birth mother counseling designed to increase the likelihood of an informed, intelligent adoption decision did not occur;
- prenatal testing for drug use or abuse during the pregnancy, genetic or congenital abnormalities, and other testing was not conducted (although tests will be performed on the baby while in the nursery, especially to identify recent drug exposure);
- sometimes there is little or no information on the identity of the birth father or his ethnicity, race, medical status or his awareness of the pregnancy, or even how many potential birth fathers might exist; and
- inadequate knowledge or information regarding the family medical, psychological, psychiatric, or other background of either of the birth parents.

When the "drop-in" situation presents itself, the agency or attorney must go into high gear to get a lot of things done in a short period of time. A meeting with the birth mother is promptly held, and she is initially advised of her right to counsel which will be provided to her at no cost should she elect to be represented by counsel.

The next step includes the completion of the various forms, statements, affidavits, and background informational questionnaires which would normally already have been done had she been working with the agency or attorney earlier in the pregnancy. It is during this time together that the agency tries to make a professional but nonmedical assessment as to the birth mother's psychological and emotional fitness to make the decision to place the baby for adoption.

Copies of all documents are explained and reviewed in detail and left with the birth mother, and she is encouraged to review them and ask questions to us or to her own legal counsel about anything she doesn't understand. If the situation appears to warrant it, and at such time is appropriate, a consent signing will be arranged with witnesses, a notary public, as prescribed by the state adoption law, and with a court reporter present.

While all of this is happening, if applicable, the hospital's social worker or case manager is injected into the process to be sure that the birth mother has an independent person with whom to consult. The hospital social worker or case manager can assess the birth mother's capacity or ability to proceed with the adoption process, even though the assessment will be made on relatively scant information. It is common for a birth mother making this 24th-hour adoption decision to feel removed from her friends and family and to be unwilling to consult with them about this very important event. Although not her legal advocate, the hospital social worker or case manager can be a very useful tool in informing the birth mother of the support and resources available to her. In addition, the birth mother should be offered immediate counseling to assist her in making her decision.

It is not uncommon for the birth mother to receive external pressures from her friends and/or family. Sometimes she's being pressured to place the baby, but more often she's being pressured to keep it. We, especially as guys who have never ourselves delivered a baby, cannot imagine the grief the birth mother must be going through with her decision, and the extent to which that grief is exacerbated by these external pressures. Oftentimes the pressure to keep the baby – as opposed to place it for adoption – is made by family and friends for whom there would be no real responsibility to care for the child on a daily basis if indeed she choose not to place. Other times family, friends, and clergy, with the best of intentions, simply think they're doing the right thing, and that the placement is being made out of desperation and will be immediately and permanently regretted by the birth mother.

It's not for us to say whether she should keep or place, but suffice it to say this: If a woman goes to the hospital and delivers a baby, and she is seriously considering placing that baby for permanent adoption with strangers, there is something going on in her life and with her situation that demands a very close examination before the tremendous responsibility of parenthood to a newborn should be seriously considered.

Sometimes birth mothers consider meeting with a prospective adoptive family prior to deciding whether to place, and sometimes they trust the professionals' judgment as to which family should be chosen to adopt the child. Our experience has been that the birth mother is most anxious just to know that the baby she just delivered is going to be in a stable family and she more often than not relies on the adoption professionals to accomplish that goal. Thus, a meeting with the prospective adoptive family is often declined and a description of the family is generally the extent to which the birth mother wants to participate in the process of being matched with a family.

After the agency's or attorney's initial meeting with the birth mother, a prospective adoptive family is contacted and fully informed of the opportunity as well as the risks of not having any history or prior working relationship with the birth mother. If they choose to be matched with her and proceed with the adoption, the necessary paperwork is promptly prepared and we proceed to the execution of consent papers with the birth mother. Filings are promptly made to notify the court of the match and to file the appropriate petitions with the court including the petition for the termination of parental rights. Simultaneously, a search is done of the putative father registry to see if anyone has filed a claim of paternity of the child. The adoption is now on a fast-track. The prospective adoptive family will visit with the baby in the nursery until discharged and everything else from that point forward is similar to the conventional non– "drop-in" adoption.

Our experience has been that, notwithstanding the lack of prenatal care and the inability to know for certain where the birth mother has been or what she's been doing (or exposed to) during the pregnancy, most families are excited about the "drop-in" situation. To date our results with these situations have been excellent.

It is unusual, in our experience, for a birth mother who is involved in a "drop-in" adoption scenario to request pictures, letters, or other information about the child going forward. In most cases, it seems as if she has made a conscious decision to close this chapter of her life and move on knowing that she has made the decision that benefits the baby most.

CHAPTER

4

"Open" and "Closed" Adoptions

We are often asked by prospective adoptive families and birth parents whether we do open adoptions, closed adoptions, or both. We hear terms such as "semi-open," "semi-closed," and every permutation you can imagine. The terms "open adoption" and "closed adoption" have different meanings to different people and neither term exists in Florida's adoption laws. But since the question is asked so frequently, let's try to explain at least our interpretation of the terms.

A "closed adoption" is one in which the biological parents and the prospective adoptive family don't meet, don't know each other's names, don't know where each other lives, and have no contact. The reasoning behind this from the birth parent(s)' perspective is that they want to close the chapter dealing with what may be called an unplanned and or unwanted pregnancy and move forward with their lives. Being assured of their anonymity goes a long way toward achieving that goal. Further, it enables the birth parents to gain a level of assurance that their lives will be protected from an invasion of their privacy by the child they placed for adoption and/or the child's adoptive parents in the future.

An "open adoption" is one which includes the meeting of the birth parent(s) and the prospective adoptive family before the child is born and involves contact at the time of delivery and even after the adoption is finalized in court. It can include participation in birthday parties of the child and holiday celebrations as well as other fact-to-face visits and can range from one to many annual visits.

As times change, what used to be a closed adoption is now approaching a level of semi-open adoption in which there is some level of communication between the birth parents and the prospective adoptive family usually only before or at the time of the birth of the baby. The level of openness is almost always driven by the birth parents and can include contact ranging from one or more face-to-face meetings before birth to the prospective adoptive family going to medical appointments and sometimes including the presence of the prospective adoptive family at the delivery of the baby. Although a bit uncommon, a birth parent may request a prospective adoptive parent to cut the umbilical cord at the delivery. Depending on the agreement, postdelivery contact can include family get-togethers after the adoption is finalized or simply an occasional visit or no personal contact at all which we find is the more frequent request.

The issue often plays out somewhat differently in real life than it does on paper. Jeff has handled a handful of mediations in which birth parents and adoptive families have dramatically different visions of what they agreed to in their written or verbal postdelivery contact agreement, when there is one. Childless couples who are so close to completing an adoption that they can smell it will agree to just about anything. Biweekly Facetime calls for the first year to update the birth mother on the status of the baby? Really!?!? First of all, does biweekly mean twice a week or once every two weeks? Answer: Either one, so you'd better be clear as to which you're agreeing to. Next, why would the adoptive family want to be beholden to having to call the birth mother to give her updates? She just placed the baby voluntarily for permanent adoption, not for babysitting! What if the birth mother doesn't like what she sees and hears? Does she get input into the raising of the child? She already made her parenting decision, which was to allow this family to take and parent this child forever. Why would she think it would be healthy to hang on to the situation any longer?

I mediated a case in which the adoptive family agreed to allow the birth mother to visit the baby one weekend per month for the first year of the baby's life, and then once every two months every year thereafter. This was written down and signed by both birth parents and the birth mother. In their excitement about adopting the baby, the family forgot to imagine the practical application of this promise. They lived in the same state but approximately six hours away from the birth mother! Who was to pay for her transportation and accommodations for these visits? When the time came for the first visit, these issues came to light very quickly. The birth mother asked them to wire money for gas, and they did. She even asked them for, and actually received from them, reimbursement for her lost wages for not being able to work for the weekend!

She drove to their home with bag in hand, expecting to stay in their home, their private sanctuary from the trials and tribulations of the world, for the weekend. This to me is not a visit so much as a home invasion. The LAST thing this couple of new parents needed immediately after taking their child home from the hospital was this woman moving into their home, presumably to judge their ability to raise their new child! On top of it all, the birth mother, of course, expected to be fed and entertained when she was done playing with the newborn baby. In essence, these people had just adopted a newborn and a selfish and immature adult.

This lasted for a few visits, but it wasn't long before the family had enough. They insisted to this woman that she attend a mediation to renegotiate the postdelivery contact or they would simply outright cancel it and take the chance that she'd attempt to have it enforced in court.

The issues were fleshed out during the mediation and a new agreement was written, this time with the benefit of a party looking at the situation through a lens of reality.

As stated, the degree of openness after birth depends primarily on the desire of the birth parent(s). Some want periodic information about the child's progress to assure themselves of the child's well-being, and some find it extremely difficult to deal with a feeling of loss and need to be involved in the child's life for some time going forward. There is certainly no right or wrong approach; rather, the level of contact is based on the various elements agreed to between the parties.

With technology moving so quickly and social media being embraced by so many people, the concept of complete privacy is rapidly evolving and seemingly deteriorating. If an adoptive family posts information on a social media platform, they cannot expect the level of privacy that would exist without the posting. The other side of that coin is that the family may be so happy to have adopted that their need to tell the world overwhelms their concerns about possible unexpected contact from the birth parents. It should be noted that the existence and/or degree of openness and adoptions is sometimes governed by state law. When crafting an adoption plan, one must never overlook the primary consideration – what's in the best interest of the child.

CAUTION

If complying with an agreement with the birth parents to provide contact with the adopted child becomes problematic, the adoptive parents need to seek legal advice to determine if not complying is an option or if they need to follow a formal legal path.

A much more complicated issue is the enforceability of "open adoption" arrangements, or of written or verbal postdelivery contact agreements or plans in general. That, too, is a function of state law and is usually the product of court cases interpreting the laws as opposed to state adoption statutes.

In short, if an adoptive family enters into an agreement that is presented to them by the birth mother and they know from the outset that they have no intention of performing their end of the agreement but they know that if they say they agree the birth mother will place the baby with them, then they have just defrauded the birth mother into consenting to the adoption, and such fraud may act to invalidate the consent. On the other hand, if they fully intend to perform their promise, but it becomes unreasonable, impossible, or outside the best interest of the child to do so, they *may* be able to fail or refuse to perform their promise without jeopardizing the adoption. In the latter case, there was not a lie told just to convince the birth mother to consent to the adoption, there was an honest change in circumstances. Therefore, the birth mother would likely have no recourse as to the adoption. However, before you decide to take a step in this direction, we URGE you to consult with your adoption attorney, as laws will vary and even the smallest facts may change the chemistry of the hypothetical!

In our experience, families prefer the closed or at most semi-open adoption as they feel that future contact may be emotionally difficult to both the birth parents and the adoptive family and can certainly cause much confusion in the years to come for the child.

CHAPTER

5

Services Provided by Adoption Agencies and Attorneys to Adoptive Parents

Adoption services are customarily provided by a state-licensed adoption agency or an adoption attorney licensed to practice law in the state where the adoption is to take place.

Agency Adoptions

As we have said, every state has unique laws, rules, and regulations which govern the placement of children for adoption by agencies which are licensed, regulated, overseen, audited by, and answerable to a state licensing authority.

The adoption agency typically orchestrates the process by arranging with the birth parent(s) and the prospective adoptive family to place the child in the home of the prospective adoptive family after the birth and after the execution of legal consent papers by the birth mother and, when required, the birth father. The agency customarily coordinates the signing of these essential and crucial papers through its legal counsel.

Once consent is given in the manner prescribed by law and by the parties whose consent is required, the agency typically becomes the legal guardian of the child until either the birth parents' legal rights to the child are terminated or, depending upon the state where the adoption takes place, until the final hearing in court takes place at which time the prospective adoptive family becomes the child's legal parents and the agency's responsibility as legal guardian is extinguished.

An agency will evaluate prospective adoptive parents before accepting them as clients. Don't think you are being singled out; this is a normal procedure and is mandated by most state licensing authorities.

Once a prospective adoptive family has been thoroughly vetted, reviewed, and accepted by an agency, the process of looking for the right match begins. This process involves the agency identifying birth parents who express an interest in placing a child, born or as-yet unborn, for adoption with the prospective adoptive family identified by the agency with or without any input from the birth parent(s). Some birth parents want to take an active role in family selection, and others choose not to do so. The extent, if any, of such involvement is entirely in the hands of the birth parent(s).

The agency, guided by its attorneys, will make decisions regarding compliance with the laws about whose consents are required to complete the adoption and when, where, and how consents may be secured, among many other legal issues.

Services Typically Provided to Prospective Adoptive Families

The following services, in one form or another, are often provided by adoption agencies:

- Meeting with the prospective adoptive family to advise them of the generic details of the adoption process to include a detailed discussion of the risks, both financial and emotional, and the rewards of a successful adoption along with a best guess of the approximate time needed to match the prospective adoptive family with the adoption situation that suits them best, court procedures, operating practices of the agency, and the projected costs involved in an adoption. To do so we arrange a two- or three-hour meeting necessary to explain to the family the entire process of adoption to enable them to understand the legal, social, economic, emotional, and psychological issues of an adoption on a face-to-face basis. Our agency's meetings are not group meetings or seminars. We meet with clients personally and privately.
- Provide counseling regarding the availability of local support groups attended by other prospective adoptive parents and suggest a list of books written specifically for families in the preadoption stage of their lives to answer questions and provide additional general information about the process.
- Evaluate the family's adoption application to assure that all of the adoption agency's criteria have been met, including the prospective adoptive family's perceived capacity to give and receive affection, its ability to provide for the child's physical, financial and emotional needs, and a determination that the prospective adoptive family members are in total agreement with the adoption plan and understand the expectations and restrictions surrounding the process of adoption.

- Arrange for (if necessary) and carefully evaluate the prospective adoptive family's home study to assure that it meets the requirements set forth by the state as well as the agency in order to place a newborn baby or an older child in the home as well as to determine the ethnicity, age, health status, and/or sex of the child that is perceived by the social work experts to be the best match for the family.
- Contact with named personal references for the adoptive family as a further confirmation that the family's stability and readiness for either a first child or brother or sister to another child or children already in the home.
- Arrange and conduct any meetings required by the attorneys for the prospective adoptive family to cover and discuss all legal issues relating to the prospective adoption.
- Prepare informational statements pertaining to birth parent(s) to assist the prospective adoptive families in evaluating backgrounds of birth parents to determine whether or not a specific match is appropriate and/or acceptable to the family.
- Counsel and educate in preparation for the adoption case, whether it be successful or not.
- Carefully select or recommend and match the prospective adoptive family with a birth parent(s) who appears to be a good fit for the family.
- Provide the family with all of the birth mother's available medical records, including history, progress charts, medical notes, laboratory blood work results, and diagnostic imaging reports, among others, as they become available during the case.
- Provide the family with available social, genetic, and medical information for the birth father, if he is known or part of the plan.
- Identify medical procedures required by health-care providers for the health and safety of the birth mother and the unborn baby.
- Advise adoptive family of medical and, when applicable, mental health appointments to then be followed by physical copies of redacted medical records and correspondence relative to such appointments.
- Dialogue with family to discuss physical and psychological needs of the birth mother as she encounters challenges in her pregnancy.
- Provide counseling and moral support to the prospective adoptive family by discussing fears and apprehensions as the weeks and months pass.
- Following the acceptance of the match by both the family and the birth parent(s), arrange and supervise any and all phone calls, emails, and personal meetings requested by the birth parent(s) and/or prospective adoptive parents and advise, prepare, and counsel the prospective adoptive family as to the issues that may become part of those calls or meetings and coordinate of any meetings or phone contacts between the birth parent(s) and the adoptive family to ease as well as control the fluidity of the meeting or phone calls.
- Discuss with the prospective adoptive family the necessity for postdelivery communication with the birth parent(s), including providing written

updates and photographs upon request of the birth parent(s), at reasonable intervals, and to facilitate the delivery of pictures and update letters.

- Generate, through its attorneys, all of the legal documents necessary under state law to be completed by the prospective adoptive family for the court's review.
- Arrange and advise as to plans made for the birth mother to be admitted to the hospital, or, alternatively, help create the plan whereby she can safely and efficiently get to the hospital at such time as she goes into labor.
- If applicable, advise the adoptive family of requirements to obtain ICPC (Interstate Compact on the Placement of Children) approvals from both the sending and receiving states.
- Arrange for communication between the birth parent(s) and the prospective adoptive family and the hospital to facilitate the family's visit with the birth mother in the recovery area (when appropriate) and/or the baby in the nursery.
- If the adoptive family resides in another state, communicate with their home study agency in order to collect, review, and compile all required additional documents, including personal reference letters, local police background checks, current medical health records from the adoptive family's health-care providers, home study updates, and fingerprint records to enable the filing of necessary documents with the court.
- Inform the family's out-of-state agency of the number of postplacement visits necessary to be completed to comply with the law of the state with jurisdiction over the adoption.
- Secure assurances that all required services will be provided by the out-of-state agency to the adoptive family on a postplacement basis.
- After birth, apply for state-funded subsidies for a child born with special needs as defined by applicable state law and applying for a newborn birth certificate for the baby as well as applying for Social Security number and Medicaid, where needed.
- Where necessary, assemble all required interstate documentation from birth parents, the adoptive family, the health-care providers, the court, and others for the purpose of preparation of the interstate adoption application package for the sending and receiving states and the timely filing of the interstate adoption application.
- Respond to requests for additional information from the sending or receiving state's administrative staff and comply with interstate rules and regulations to enable a favorable determination on the interstate application.
- Follow up on the status of interstate filings.
- Confer with the adoptive family to advise of additional requests from the interstate sending or receiving states to obtain approval, thus permitting the adopting family to return to their home state with the child.
- Assist agency's attorney in the termination of parental rights proceeding and in the process of finalization of the adoption.
- Apply for any needed subsidies for the adopted baby; and if necessary, work with the attorneys to secure an order amending the initial birth certificate to

assist in securing a passport in the child's postadoption name for travel outside of the United States prior to the final hearing of adoption and/or for a Medicaid or financial subsidy for children with "special needs."

The following services may be provided by the agency's attorneys:

- Evaluation of the birth parent(s') information to determine the legality of the proposed adoption.
- Determination of identity of the parties whose consent and/or other affidavits must be secured.
- Draft, finalize, and oversee execution of birth parent questionnaires, adoption disclosure statements, acknowledgment of receipt of pre- and postbirth disclosure statements, waivers of venue, prebirth affidavits concerning paternity, affidavits pertaining to out-of-state placements, request for financial support, Indian Child Welfare Act Affidavits, consents for birth mother and/or birth father and/or legal father, other affidavits needed from either of the birth parents or, when applicable, legal parent, acknowledgment of receipt of copies of documents by the birth parent(s), statements identifying all possible fathers of the pregnancy, and such other documents as the particular proposed adoption requires.
- Additionally, the following documents will likely become a part of the process: adoption placement agreement with the prospective adoptive family, projected costs of adoption, risks of adoption agreement with the prospective adoptive family, at-risk agreement and letter of guardianship with prospective adoptive family, and such other legal documents as may be required to process an adoption proceeding in court.
- Prepare court order to permit moving forward with the proposed adoption.
- Prepare petition for termination of parental rights with all required exhibits thereto.
- Scheduling and attending hearing to terminate parental rights.
- Prepare final judgment of the court terminating parental rights.
- Prepare petition for adoption, scheduling, and attending final hearing to secure final judgment of adoption and prepare order from court approving expenses of adoption.
- Prepare application for new birth certificate for the adoptee.
- Where appropriate, perform a diligent search for the birth father; prepare publication in newspaper, when required, for birth father, and arrange for service of process to notify birth father of pending and forthcoming hearings regarding the termination of his parental rights.
- Prepare motion and court order to secure Medicaid and a Social Security number for the adoptee.

The above listings of services are not carved in stone; rather, they are the types of services which are often provided by adoption agencies and either their attorneys or the adoptive family's attorney. Again, you are reminded that each case is different and may likely have different requirements.

Attorney Adoptions

(No, we're not asking you to adopt an attorney.) A family is not limited to proceeding in search of an adoption through the facilities of a state-licensed child-placing agency. Licensed attorneys in every state are also authorized to represent families in the adoption process. In such cases, private attorneys can perform, or arrange for, the provision of almost all of the services which an adoption agency provides.

There are a couple of differences in what the attorney can provide and what the agency can provide. For example, in Florida, a private attorney does not automatically become the legal guardian of a child after required birth mother consent papers are signed after the birth of the child. The attorney is nonetheless responsible for the child until a court orders preliminary approval of the placement of the child in the home of the prospective adoptive family whereupon the prospective adoptive parents become the child's legal guardians pending finalization of the adoption. Prior to finalization, the attorney has the right and responsibility to remove the child from the home of the prospective adoptive family if deemed by the attorney to be in the child's best interests. This should be done, if and when necessary, only by court order. Further, attorneys are also excluded from making applications for things like Social Security coverage, if available, disability benefits, if available, and others forms of state and/or federal subsidies. Additionally, many attorneys do not have licensed social workers on staff to provide counseling to birth parents and prospective adoptive families, but those who don't can certainly make arrangements for such services to be provided to the birth family and to the prospective adoptive family.

Attorneys handling private adoptions generally can and do (i) assist in identifying and qualifying prospective adoptive families and birth parents; (ii) arrange counseling for birth parents and families; (iii) oversee the process of securing all required consents and other documents necessary to file in court to process the adoption case; (iv) give advice pertaining to the legal risks associated with adoptions; (v) assist in securing an agreement between the prospective adoptive family and the birth parent(s) relating to communications, if any, during all stages of the adoption process, including postdelivery contacts; (vi) prepare all required legal petitions, motions, court orders, and other documents necessary to complete the adoption in court; and, among others, (vii) focus on the fundamental premise on which all adoptions are based – doing what's in the best interest of the child.

CHAPTER 6

Working with an Adoption Agency

As a prospective adoptive parent, what can you expect when working with an adoption agency or attorney?

First, the significant legal issues associated with adoption should be covered in some detail both in general and as they may relate to the family's specific case. The prospective adoptive family should know that adoption is a creature of state law and it is thus closely governed and regulated by the court and legislative body of each state. Generally, complying with the law should not be difficult, but there is little or no margin for error. One small slipup might result in anything from undue delay and additional costs to the adoptive family all the way up to loss of the custody of the child. So, have a discussion about the effect of the law of the state where you adopt as well as the law of the state where you reside, if different.

From your perspective as a prospective adoptive family, it is critical to feel comfortable with and confident in the people to whom you are entrusting such a significant event in your life, not to mention a significant amount of your financial resources. It has always been our agency's policy to deliver an unvarnished full and fair discussion of the process from the time of the first meeting with the various parties to the finalization of the adoption and beyond.

The prospective adoptive family should be informed as to the agency's views toward families that already have one or more children. Some agencies and birth parents are adverse to such placements, wanting the child to be the first child adopted by the family. Further, it is important to know if the agency will consider the family's preference of gender as to the child sought to be adopted.

The level and frequency of communication between the family and the agency is yet another important discussion. Will the family be provided with initial and ongoing prenatal records, hospital reports, laboratory reports, ultrasound reports, and other available medical information? Will there be an opportunity to meet with the birth parent(s) and, if so, when and under what circumstances? It is also important that a family know who in the agency will have primary responsibility for overseeing the legal, financial, social, medical, counseling, and other aspects of the adoption and that the family has ready access to such person(s).

Some adoptive families are "higher-maintenance" than others, and feel as if there's something wrong if they're not hearing updates from the agency twice a day. Other adoptive families are content to receive a once- or twice-weekly call, along with medical records as they become available. The conversation regarding the family's needs and expectations is best had right up front when unrealistic expectations can be addressed before they become a problem.

> **TIP**
>
> As a prospective adoptive parent, it's important that you feel comfortable with your adoption agency and that the agency fully discloses all aspects of the adoption process at the outset. You shouldn't have to ask.

For example, our agency's policy is to make ourselves available to every birth parent 24/7/365. We have chargers for our chargers. Neither of us has ever seen a movie start to finish without being interrupted. We probably have melon-sized tumors behind our left front pockets.

When it comes to adoptive parents, however, we prefer to make ourselves available from 9 to 5, Mondays through Fridays, unless of course there is an emergency or the birth is actually imminent. Adoptive families are the clients, and they're the ones paying the bills, but generally speaking they don't have the same emergent needs as the women who are pregnant.

From an adoption agency's perspective, it is important to have a high level of confidence that the family has a realistic expectation of the agency's services and of the process, including the risks of an adoption. The family should clearly understand that the agency is an active participant in the process but cannot guarantee its outcome and, among others, that the agency cannot guarantee a "perfect baby" or that the birth parent(s) or some other party won't try to scuttle the adoption at any time. The agency has to know that both parents are equally committed to the adoption process and that one is not grudgingly proceeding to appease the other. It happens!!

At the meeting with the prospective adoptive family, the agency should inquire into areas such as criminal history, bankruptcies, employment stability, prior marriages, other children of prior marriages, and whether any court orders relative to those children (e.g., child support) have been violated, general health, education, and the like. While this will all be part of the family's home study, it may be that the presence of some of these factors suggests that an application with the agency should not be pursued.

Most families with whom we meet are in good standing on these and all other issues. While most families going into the adoption process want to focus only on the positives, we feel it's critical to have an open discussion of the negatives. The negatives are basically the medical risks (unhealthy pregnancy and baby), miscarriage, stillbirth, as well as the other risks such as the birth parents changing their mind or withdrawing from the process for any reason, including, regrettably, adoption deception, as outlined in more detail elsewhere herein.

We spend a good amount of time painting a realistic picture of the world of adoption, not so much from a textbook point of view but rather from a hands-on view in which what is sometimes not in the books becomes the adoption reality and sometimes the adoption nightmare. We are not social workers or nuns, and we (mainly Jeff) have been accused of presenting a worst-case scenario regarding every step of the process. Yet despite this, some of the smartest and most successful people in the world have chosen to proceed and have adopted through our services.

The agency representative should very frankly discuss the fact that not every baby is born in good health. Birth mothers sometimes abuse themselves and their unborn babies with drugs or engage in other activities which expose themselves and the baby they are carrying to risks during the pregnancy. It is important to discuss with the prospective adoptive family that even a woman who takes exceptionally good care of herself (no drugs, no drinking, no smoking, good diet, prenatal vitamins, exercise, and attends all medical visits) can deliver a baby with problems ranging from minor to major. Basically, the family needs to know that nothing guarantees a healthy baby.

Before meeting with an adoption agency or attorney, it is essential that the family do some due diligence and learn as much as possible about the history and experience of the agency and its principles. That information will generally be available from the state's licensing authority and/or an Internet search. Don't believe everything you read, however, without following it up with some research of your own.

Discussions with other families who have previously adopted through the agency are strongly encouraged. Our experience is that most adoptive families are enthusiastic about discussing their experiences with families beginning the adoption process. That enthusiasm should be taken advantage of by prospective adoptive families.

Anyone can look good on paper or on a website but the initial meeting is where the rubber meets the road. The agency and the family may realize at such a meeting that they are not a good fit for each other and can therefore save time, money, and aggravation by moving in a different direction. There may be certain attributes of the personnel with whom the family would be working that make the relationship incompatible. By the same token, the agency may feel that it would be inappropriate to work with the family for one or more reasons that would not necessarily be determinable easily from a written application. For example, a prospective adoptive family may have the unrealistic expectation that every baby will be in perfect health and cute enough for the cover of a baby magazine, but that's just not how the world of adoption works. Just as it is true with the birth of a biological child, there can be no assurance given as to the perfect health of a child born and placed for adoption. Alternatively, the family may not like something about the communication style or some other facet of the agency, or may not feel confident in the agency's ability to execute the family's adoption plan the way they want it done. Either way, nothing personal, there are many other agencies and attorneys from which the family can choose.

Example: A very nice family was referred to us and made an appointment to come in to meet in person. The family told us from the outset that they wanted a "Christian adoption." At this point the agency had been doing adoptions for over 10 years, yet we were unaware as to what made an adoption Christian or otherwise. Two of the principals of the agency are Jewish, but the agency is not a "Jewish agency," nor does it do "Jewish adoptions," whatever that might mean. The family was dead set on having what they called a "Christ-centered" adoption agency, and we had to tell them that they came to the wrong place. We would have been happy to work with them, but we clearly did not meet their criteria.

The family should check the state licensing authority to determine whether there have been complaints filed against the agency and, if so, the frequency and nature of the complaints and their disposition. You can't please all of the people all of the time, and having a complaint or two does not automatically mean that you're not doing a great job. Not all adoptions have successful conclusions, and families which have suffered disappointments occasionally blame the agency for failing to properly process the adoption or for neglecting to take steps necessary to promote the successful completion of the adoption, even when they know full well that the failure of the adoption was not the fault of the agency.

If there are any questions which arise from your investigation, you should not hesitate to seek a thorough response to your concerns from the agency. The agency's failure to provide a reasonable explanation should be given the appropriate amount of weight by the family when ultimately choosing an adoption agency.

It is important to know the agency's regulatory history, and it is equally or more important for the prospective adoptive family to speak with other families that have been involved in the adoption process with the agency. Again, websites and promotional materials are nice, but nothing beats personal referrals, experiences, and endorsements. This area should be seriously pursued, and it is common for the adoption agency to give the names of willing adoptive families so you can inquire as to their experience with the agency. With that said, the reality is that the agency is really only going to give you the names and contact information of their happiest and most satisfied clients, obviously, but it's still nice to hear someone's perspective.

> **TIP**
>
> If you feel very comfortable with a particular agency, but discover there has been a complaint or two filed against them, you should simply ask the principals about the complaints. Sometimes complaints have substance; sometimes not.

With very rare exceptions, our agency only works by personal referral, so by the time of family contacts us to set up a meeting, they likely have heard of one or more family's experiences and thus come into the meeting with a higher level of knowledge and confidence in the agency. The effect of this fact is to make the meeting more productive because the prospective adoptive family can focus on the process rather than spend time trying to measure the level of confidence they have in the agency. We cannot emphasize enough the importance of contacting other families and, when possible, contacting an agency to whom you are directly referred by an excellent referral source. It makes the process much smoother from the get-go.

CHAPTER

7

Services Provided to Birth Parents by Agencies

The following services will generally be made available to the birth mother and, when applicable, the birth father or legal father. Some of the services listed below will be overseen by the agency's attorneys, and others will be provided directly by the agency representatives.

Adoption agencies generally provide the following services, among others, to the birth parent(s):

- Assist in securing safe, secure, and affordable living arrangements (preplacement and postplacement, as permitted by law).
- Arrange for utility services and payment of utility bills (gas, electric, cell phone, water, sewer, etc.).
- Arrange for medical doctor and laboratory appointments and secure and review all reports from health-care providers, including obstetrician's medical reports, ultrasound reports, progress chart notes, medical histories, laboratory results, diagnostic imaging reports, and such other medical information as is available about the pregnancy.
- Schedule and coordinate family counseling services for the birth mother and/or the birth father with agency and/or outside professionals.
- Arrange transportation to and from all necessary medical, dental, laboratory, counseling, and other appointments.
- Arrange for hospital registration and negotiation of payment for hospital and physician billings.
- Review all charges relating to the birth mother and the baby.

- Determine possible eligibility for Medicaid or other forms of medical insurance or other coverage and assistance, where applicable, and provide services to acquire and maintain such coverage in effect during all applicable periods of time during and after the pregnancy.
- Forward redacted health-care provider reports to the prospective adoptive family.
- Respond, as appropriate and as permitted by law, to financial requests of birth mother, including foreseen as well as unforeseen expenses during and sometimes after the pregnancy.
- Review the genetic background questionnaires completed by the birth parent(s) and, as appropriate, follow up to secure the most complete information available.
- Assist birth parent(s) in dealing with questions regarding adoption issues as they relate to them and their families.
- Arrange and field calls on a variety of matters from the birth parent(s) about prebirth activities, hospitalization, and postdelivery events inclusive of discharge and postdischarge issues.
- Discuss step-by-step process associated with birth mother's admission to the hospital, delivery, discharge, execution of consents/surrenders, waivers, affidavits, and other documentation relative to the adoptive placement of the child and court proceedings pertaining thereto.
- Arrange the flow of communications after birth, if applicable, between and among the adoptive family, the birth mother, the birth father, and the adoption agency.
- Discuss reasons for the placement of the child for adoption.
- Assess effects of the proposed adoption on the birth parent(s) and, perhaps, their family, including any young children they may already be parenting.
- Communicate with birth parent(s) regarding fulfillment of any agreed-upon postdelivery communications and exchanges of information, including providing pictures, progress reports, and holiday exchanges to and from birth parent(s) and adoptive family for a generally agreed-upon time, if any such arrangement is made.
- Arrange and pay for postdelivery counseling sessions, including arrangements for transportation to and from such sessions.
- Arrange and process of postdelivery maintenance and support payments for birth mother's living expenses, as permitted by law.
- Communicate with the birth parent(s) regarding issues dealing with the execution of consents, surrenders, affidavits, waivers, and other statements required by state law and/or the agency.
- Discuss, when appropriate, arrangements for the adoptive family to be present at the time of the delivery and arrange with the hospital's case management or social services department for access to the nursery by the adoptive family to commence the very important bonding process and to facilitate the free flow of information regarding the progress of the newborn and discharge details.

- Arrange and prepare for any in-person meetings among the birth parent(s), the prospective adoptive family, and the agency, if requested by the birth parent(s).
- Assist the birth mother in securing job training, employment, educational (e.g., GED) programs or other forms of personal advancement activities leading to the ultimate goal of self-sufficiency for the birth mother following the birth of the baby, if permitted by state law.
- Arrange for the payment of the birth mother's reasonable and necessary living expenses to the providers of necessary items of support, including rent, utilities, transportation expenses, medications as well as reasonable costs associated with postdelivery doctor visits and transportation therefore as permitted by state law.
- Arrange for basic necessities to assist the birth mother in her progression through the pregnancy without the need to suffer undue stress about the unavailability of such support.

There are other services generally provided by the agency depending upon the particular circumstances which present themselves relating to the birth mothers and birth father's socioeconomic position.

Counseling for Birth Parents

When an adoption agency provides counseling to a birth family, there are important matters that should be addressed. The initial areas of concern should include the reasons that the birth parent(s) is considering not parenting the child themselves, thus giving rise to their planned adoption. Such a discussion should include the financial situation the birth mother finds herself in which includes the ability or inability to provide, among others, housing, food, clothing, transportation, and medical care to her family. Also to be discussed are issues ranging from substance abuse to employment to physical or mental health issues to relationships with other members of their families, among others.

One of the goals of the counseling sessions should be to assess how sincere the birth parents are in creating and completing an adoption plan and their perceived ability to withstand any pressure they may get from their family for having made such a plan as well as the cultural and societal pressures that may be brought to bear on them to cancel their adoption plan and keep the baby.

Other proper topics for discussion at a counseling session with birth parents include whether there are other members of the birth parent(s) family who are willing and able to care for the child and whether that would be acceptable to the birth parent(s). Of course no effort should ever be made to persuade the birth parent(s) to either surrender a child for adoption or to parent as that is ethically and morally inappropriate and may well expose an otherwise-valid adoption to revocation based on duress or coercion.

The birth parent(s) must understand the difference between foster care and adoption. They will be informed that foster care is a temporary placement of the child while they attempt to achieve certain goals which would enable them to be reunified with the child. They will also be informed that adoption is the permanent termination of all parental rights to the child with the end result being that the child becomes a full legal member of someone else's family. There should be a full exploration of the effects on the child of placing his or her child for adoption. Only when these issues are covered is it safe to conclude that the adoption choice was made knowingly, intelligently and voluntarily, and with full and fair disclosure of its impact.

Paying the Bills of the Birth Mother

It is common for birth parents to be in an economic situation where they find themselves unemployed or underemployed and thus unable to afford the costs of rent, utilities, medication, medical care, clothing, food, transportation, and such other day-to-day expenses as are typically encountered during a pregnancy. Further, if we're being honest here, some of the women who are placing babies suffer from some type of addiction, particularly to pain pills, and therefore do not and/or cannot hold down a steady job, and have a great deal of trouble earning and saving money. While it is always important for people to have a roof over their heads, food to eat, and the other necessities of life, it becomes especially important for pregnant women to have such necessities available to them throughout the pregnancy and, if necessary, for a period of time after delivery to give the birth mother time to get back on her feet and resume her role in the employment world.

So you may ask why doesn't the birth father provide these goods and services to the woman he impregnated? The simple answers are that if his identity is known, he, too, may be unemployed or underemployed for a variety of reasons including his inability to qualify for a job or his decision to simply not work and live off of the funding provided to the birth mother by the adoption agency or attorney who is essentially spending the prospective adoptive family's money.

Here's the bottom line: in the thousands of adoptions we have been involved in, we estimate that *in almost every situation,* the birth mother required some degree of financial assistance from the adoption agency (using, of course, the prospective adoptive family's money). In almost all of those cases, the birth father, whether known or unknown, was not interested in even attempting to support the birth mother during the pregnancy. That's a hard, cold fact. If that sounds outrageous, we agree. While you may find this to be somewhat cynical, the fact is that in almost all of the adoption cases we have worked on, the known birth father has contributed next to nothing financially to the birth mother whether he was living with her or not. There have been exceptions, but those have been very rare and very far between, sort of like spotting Bigfoot riding a unicorn being chased by the Loch Ness Monster. That rare.

CAUTION

Even though the prospective adopting parents may pay the birth mother's expenses, there is no guarantee that a birth parent ultimately will sign the consent papers authorizing the adoption after the baby is born.

So, whatever the birth father's reasons may be, if he doesn't support the birth mother during the pregnancy, someone has to and the law in Florida permits the birth mother to receive financial assistance to pay for her reasonable and necessary needs during the pregnancy (and for up to 6 weeks after delivery under certain circumstances). Again, this is for the purpose of assisting her in getting through a pregnancy in a healthy and safe manner and having time to recover and reenter the working world.

As in every area of life, there are individuals who will bend and break the rules to achieve a result that was not intended by the law. There are adoption professionals from sea to shining sea who will and do look at the ability to provide financial assistance to the birth mother as a way to "buy" the baby. They'll advertise and brag about the amount of money they can sneak through the system to the birth mother, sometimes a shady but legal way, and sometimes through neglecting to advise the court of the funds that were actually spent. Make no mistake about it – there are secret "bidding wars" that occur when savvy birth mothers pit agencies against one another to see how much they can get in the way of financial support. It is not unusual for the agencies to know that they're bidding against another, and the end result is that people of average financial means sometimes get squeezed out of the private adoption process.

It is important to state that, after paying for all of the birth mother's reasonable and necessary living expenses, there is no assurance that she will sign the required consent papers to proceed with the planned adoption.

CHAPTER
8

The Risks of Adoption

If you've made it this far into this book I don't see why you don't deserve to know a crucial fact about adoption that adoption professionals are desperately afraid to discuss publicly, and it goes like this: Domestic adoption is so rife with fraud and scams right now that I am actually surprised when one goes through without the birth mother "changing her mind" at the end and keeping the baby and the adoptive family's money.

We have spoken with adoption colleagues here in Florida who have told us that midway through the year that we've been writing this book they've done ZERO adoptions. Oh, they've had cases – sometimes 15, 20 cases – but no adoptions. That means that every one of those 15 to 20 hopeful prospective adoptive families has paid for rent, groceries, transportation, clothing, medications, utilities, not to mention legal and agency fees, only to get that heartbreaking call at the end of the day saying, "I'm so sorry, but Barbie canceled her adoption plan." Recourse: NONE.

Try again? Can they afford it financially and/or emotionally? I don't mind telling you that I would not be able to compose myself if I were on the receiving end of that call, because not only does the family have to find a way to move on, but they also know that the baby, who was theirs as far as they were concerned, will now likely have a less-than-stellar life with a MUCH less-than-stellar person.

What's worse than that? Here you go: How about if the birth mother whom you've been supporting for the past 6 months at the end cancels the adoption, keeps the baby, and then "sells" it to another agency or family, claiming that she owes "back rent" and other back expenses? She accepts support from *you* during the entire pregnancy, then places the baby with another family in exchange for a big fat check

49

to cover those expenses which you already covered out of your very own posttax hard-working pocket. We caught one doing that, but didn't have enough evidence to get the courts or law enforcement to take any action against her.

Birth mothers, birth mother advocates, and even some adoption professionals will hate us for revealing this truth. They'll say things like "That woman is the mother of that baby until and unless she decides to give it up for adoption!" and they'd be absolutely right. The "system" is so stacked up against the adoptive families as opposed to the birth mothers that we continue to find it hard to believe that anyone would expose themselves to this kind of risk.

How Do You Know If a Birth Mother Is Scamming?

You never do! Birth parent scams come in all levels of sophistication. Some of the ones that are small-time and very effective when used against hopeful prospective adoptive families listing their adoption desires on the Internet are far too unsophisticated to fool a seasoned adoption professional. The most effective scams are the easiest and least complicated.

Example One: We've heard this story over and over again. Adoptive families who are attempting to market themselves and locate birth mothers directly over the Internet, foregoing the safety net provided by an experienced adoption professional get burned with this one all the time. The alleged birth mother is in her last trimester of the pregnancy, already having contractions, and was just locked out of a motel for failure to pay the room rate. She suddenly realizes that she does not want to keep the baby. The caller will swear she doesn't want the baby but will only work with the family if money is wired to her to pay for the room for another week so she and her kids won't be out in the cold. Oh, and don't forget to include the grocery money.

Example Two: This one is foolproof and sadly it happens frequently. The birth mother goes through the entire process, knowing that she is not placing the baby for adoption, but wanting the financial support that she knows she can receive from an adoptive family. She contacts an agency or attorney, knowing that the families who can afford to take that route can also afford the "premium" support she demands. She demands and receives financial support to the point where she's living like a queen, relatively speaking. The baby is born, and she "changes her mind" and "decides" to keep the baby. Done. No recourse, game over.

Other Risks

There are many risks associated with adoption. We've already discussed birth parent deception and fraud. Other risks include, but are certainly not limited to, the following:

- Possible miscarriage or stillbirth
- Possible "change of mind" by the birth parent(s) at any time up to and including the birth of the child and, in some states, even after the birth of

the child and even after the child is placed in the physical custody of the prospective adoptive family

- The possibility of a drug-exposed child or a child born with a physical or medical issue not otherwise expected
- The various issues and concerns related by the identity of the biological father of the pregnancy, and the real-life impact of the birth mother either not knowing or refusing to identify that party
- The rights, if any, of any grandparents of the child, and the practical considerations of how those grandparents might react to their grandchild being placed for permanent adoption
- The possibility that the child is of Native American heritage and is thus unavailable for adoption absent the consent of the Native American tribe in which the child may be eligible for membership

This is not a comprehensive and exhaustive list of all possible risks. Each adoption situation comes with its own unique risks and each risk can involve emotional and financial loss.

CHAPTER 9

The Home Study

With limited exceptions, a study of the prospective adoptive family and their home is required by all states' laws before a family can be approved to adopt a child. This study is referred to as the "home study," and it is used for a variety of purposes including identifying suitable and qualified families and rooting out prospective adoptive families which are not suitable or qualified to adopt a child. It is used to help a prospective adoptive family become aware of the necessary steps that must be successfully completed in order to be approved for adoption, and it also serves as a valuable tool in educating a family as to what can be expected when and if a child is placed in their home for adoption.

The home study is also a vehicle for the agency and the court to assess and evaluate a family's understanding of the risks and rewards of adoption. Further, it is also a tool to ascertain the strengths and weaknesses of the family as well as a way to understand their expectations of life after adoption.

If the prospective adopter is a relative of the child, a home study may not be necessary, but this varies from state to state.

As with many issues in the world of adoption, home study requirements vary from state to state. The areas that may be included in the home study include, but are not limited to, the following:

- The general health of all household members
- The status of biological and other children in the household
- The motivation for adoption
- The maturity levels of the prospective adoptive family
- The family's general financial status
- The ability to provide financial support for all members of the household without the need for public assistance
- The attitudes of family members toward the prospect of welcoming an adopted child into the family
- The family's views about disciplining children
- The ability to express love and affection to a child
- The ability to provide for a child's physical and emotional needs
- The employment history of adoptive family
- The plans for child care
- The educational history of adoptive family
- The personal references from nonrelatives
- The home and neighborhood environment
- The home fire safety and evacuation considerations
- The religious beliefs and activities of the family
- The ability to deal with the stress, anxiety, and frustrations of being a parent
- The family's plan to discuss, at an appropriate time, the fact that the child was adopted and if and how that effects the child's relationship with the parents or siblings, whether biological or adopted
- The relationship of the prospective adoptive parents with their siblings, parents, and other relatives
- The legal status of the family (litigation or other legal entanglements)
- The expectations of the family insofar as health and other issues of an adoptee are concerned
- The age, ethnicity, racial, gender, and other background aspects of an adoptee
- Among others, the appointment of a legal guardian for the child in the event of a catastrophic event in the family

When we evaluate a family seeking to adopt, in addition to the above factors, we inquire about hobbies, sports, outside activities and interests, smoking habits (if any), and alcohol consumption by the prospective adoptive family. We don't mind admitting that we discriminate against smokers, and would have no problem disqualifying a family from adopting through our agency based solely on the fact that they smoke cigarettes. Same goes for any other irresponsible behavior, needless to say.

Home studies are not required in some jurisdictions when the adoptee is a relative within a certain degree of the adoptive family or where the adoptee is a stepchild or grandchild. Of course, the best bet is to seek the advice of an experienced adoption professional in your state to determine whether the relationship of the adoptee to the prospective adoptive family qualifies for an exemption from the home study requirement. You may need to pull up your state's "table of consanguinity," as discussed elsewhere in this book.

Matching Families with the Birth Parent(s)

Matching adoptive families and birth parents looks and seems relatively easy, but in reality it requires a skill set that involves several specialties, not the least of which is interpersonal communication with parties that have never given so much as a passing thought as to how to present themselves in such a way as to communicate effectively with others. This requires efficient coordination of all interested parties, and it happens tens of thousands of times yearly in the United States.

Once a family has been accepted into an adoption agency's program, the next step is generally properly educating the family as to what challenges they will be faced with as parents, especially if they have no children at the beginning of the process. Education is both available and necessary for families bringing another child into their home if they already have a biological or an adopted child. There are many resources to which an agency or attorney can direct the family to educate and prepare it for their new family dynamic, and families are usually encouraged to take parenting and similar classes as well as to secure counseling on the issues which they will hopefully soon face.

Adoptive families have commented that it's somewhat unfair that they have to jump through certain hoops when others with far less in the way of education and/or resources can have a biological child without the slightest degree of training or preparation. We agree. The law doesn't require every new parent to receive any kind of study or training, as that would be clearly unconstitutional in this country. However, those resources are available to citizens of every socioeconomic background, and are heavily promoted in government-run health clinics serving low-income pregnant women.

A great deal of thought and experience must go into the process of matching a prospective adoptive family with birth parents. For example, before an agency can even begin to create the match of prospective adoptive family and birth parents, certain facts must be known to enhance the possibility of a successful match. Specifically, the agency must understand the expectations of the birth parents for the child they intend to deliver and place for adoption as well as the expectations of the prospective adoptive family.

When we interview new birth parents, one of the areas we discuss is whether there is any interest in meeting the prospective adoptive family. If they want to meet before the birth of the child, we ask how frequently and under what circumstances. We learn whether the birth parents want the family to attend some prenatal visits and/or ultrasound appointments or whether they prefer a less invasive, less personal, and more social environment to get to know the family. In that circumstance, the meeting will likely be a lunch or dinner meeting together so that everyone can get to know more than what is written on paper about the other. We have found that meetings are well-timed by meals, with a natural beginning, middle, and end and with reasonable and natural distractions. Sitting in a room staring across a table at each other is not our preferred medium for such a meeting.

The birth parents' responses to questions of whether they want to meet range from simply wanting to get through the pregnancy and delivery without any contact with the family thus basing their acceptance of the family on the experience of and information provided by the adoption agency to a few telephone calls with the prospective adoptive family to dinners to doctors visits. There have occasionally been requests by a birth mother to have the family (usually a female member) be present in the delivery room at the time of the child's birth.

There is almost always a huge socioeconomic gap between the prospective adoptive family and the birth parent(s). One of the risks of having a meeting with the birth parent(s) and the prospective adoptive family is that the more each party knows about the other, the greater the chance is that there will be something one side doesn't like about the other and thus the process could be fragile. The other side of that coin is that the more each side likes the other, the higher the probability that the proposed adoption will be successful. It's a coin toss.

Example: We had a client who had recently sold a billion-dollar business. Money was a very important part of this couple's life, and they lived somewhat ostentatiously. No matter what the subject of the conversation, the father had a way of implicitly bragging about how much money he had. For example, when the conversation turned to sports, the father mentioned that he ran into a very successful and well-known baseball star at a bar, and they realized they had the same conspicuously displayed keychain. He didn't hesitate to mention that the keychain was made of platinum and decorated with real jewels. The value was somewhere around $25,000, which is more than the young birth couple would make in most of that year. Other than that, the adoptive couple was very pleasant and likeable, and the adoption went through just fine. Now, when I have a couple who likes to talk about their worldly possessions, I am sure to tell them to keep the bragging to a minimum in birth parent meetings.

Another area into which we make inquiry is what kind of a family the birth parents are looking for, meaning (i) do they want to be matched with a so-called "traditional" heterosexual married couple; (ii) do they want to be matched with a single parent; (iii) do they want to be matched with a same-sex couple; (iv) do they care if the family has children; (v) do they have certain age ranges in mind; and, among others, (vi) do they have specific religious or cultural characteristics with which they would be most comfortable; or do they have no specific preferences at all.

The most frequent preference by birth parents is that they want good, solid people who have the financial and emotional strength to care for the child and not abuse the child. We feel like the process works best when the birth parents leave it to us, the professionals, to make the match, with as few criteria as possible. We know our clients very well by the time it becomes time to match, and we likely already have someone in mind shortly into the first or second meeting or conversation with the birth mother.

Most agencies that we are aware of offer the birth parents biographical booklets which describe the families the agency believes will make a good match with the birth parents. The booklets generally contain what we call a "Dear Birth Mother" letter describing how excited the family is to be considered for the match and a bit of their background and interests as well as some other personal (but nonidentifying) information such as hobbies, family relationships, efforts to achieve or complete a pregnancy, and the like. The booklet also generally includes some pictures of the family engaged in family activities such as vacations, charitable events, sporting events, family get-togethers, and similar activities. Once given several of these booklets, the birth parents are asked to choose a prospective adoptive family.

Our experience is that most adoption matches are made by the birth parents with some guidance from the agency. Our personal view of making a match is that the birth parents don't really have the experience needed to read through several booklets and determine which family would make the best parents. One could argue that the birth parents are the *least* qualified people to make a match, since in many cases they have a history of being bad choice-makers. Since, in many cases, it is difficult to distinguish one family from another based on what's in the written part of the booklet, we feel that all too often the selection is based on the pictures and we do not subscribe to any theory that choosing an adoptive family through a photo album or catalog is a solid foundation on which to build an adoption. That said, however, the booklet selection process is extremely popular – just not with our agency.

To avoid the selection of a family by the birth parents essentially becoming a beauty contest, our agency has a very different approach to making a match between birth parents and a prospective adoptive family. When we interview birth parents, we listen carefully to their history, their likes and dislikes, their expectations of the aftermath of the proposed adoption, their preferences, if any, based on socioeconomic factors, ethnicity, family structure, religion, and other considerations such as whether or not they want one of the adoptive parents to be a stay-at-home parent.

Then again, there are many birth parents who simply want the adoption professionals to use their experience and their resources to identify and recommend a family for the adoption without the birth parents' input. This generally occurs because of the birth parents' recognition of the fact that this is likely their first time confronting the adoption issue and that they recognize that the agency professionals have vast experience in making matches. That said, the large majority of our adoptions are based on the agency's recommendation of a family to the birth parents after providing the details of their educational, occupational, social, medical, physical, and other attributes. In our experience and opinion, which we acknowledge differs from the opinions of many others, the birth parents don't actually want the pressure of having to review the booklets to make a choice and prefer to consider a recommendation from an experienced adoption professional.

One of the factors which a birth parent may insist on in making the match is the availability of a prospective adoptive family to attend prenatal visits with the birth parent(s). Obviously, if a birth parent wants the family to go to one or more medical appointments, or to an ultrasound or other prenatal appointment, it is impractical, but certainly not impossible, to accomplish this if the family does not live within a reasonable distance of the birth parent(s). Clearly, the birth parent(s) who wants some predelivery contact will be better served with a family whose flexible schedules and geographic location allow for them to meet as requested.

In making a match, from the agency's perspective, there are families who will meet very well with birth parents and others who we perceive will not. Those who will not meet well should not be placed in the uncomfortable position of meeting with birth parents. We feel it's best to match those families with birth parents who do not express the desire to meet the prospective adoptive family and who will rely solely on the agency's description and recommendation of the family. If no meeting is to be scheduled, the parties can always communicate by phone or through the Internet if they so desire.

The risk here, of course, is that the birth parents can change their minds about the meeting situation and want to have a personal meeting before or after the birth of the child. There is no way to avoid the situation and, like so many other aspects of adoption, this is a risk factor to be considered.

Another key factor in making a match is putting all of the facts, the good, the bad, and the ugly, on the table for each of the parties to consider. There should be no exaggerations or ambiguities. That kind of activity is not only inappropriate, but it can lead to a claim by one party or the other that they were deceived or defrauded which could undo an otherwise-successful adoption.

All aspects of the birth mother's physical, medical, and emotional status should be disclosed and the family should be encouraged to seek input from a physician of their choosing as the agency should not be in the business of giving medical advice or opinions.

In summary, the factors we think should be considered in making a match include (i) the backgrounds of each of the parties; (ii) the expectations of each of the parties; (iii) the degree to which we expect the parties to "hit it off" if and when they meet; (iv) the relationship between the specific preferences of the prospective adoptive family and of the birth parent(s); (v) the degree of risk which will be undertaken by the prospective adoptive family; and, among others, (vi) the expectation that both the birth parents and the prospective adoptive family will comply with the steps required to complete the adoption process.

Each match has its own idiosyncrasies, and each is to be crafted with great attention to detail. Of course, the goal of a good match is to have the adoption successfully completed with the birth parents feeling that they made the best plan for the child and with the adoptive family feeling that their adoption dream has come true. Superseding both of these goals is the goal of creating a match and considering and conducting the rest of the process in such a way as to promote and accomplish what is in the best interests of the child.

The Waiting Period

The waiting period is the period of time between the acceptance of a match by both the birth parent(s) and the prospective adoptive family and the delivery of the baby. No doubt this period is filled with anxiety, excitement, doubt, joy, and many other emotions. We typically refer to this period of time as a "roller-coaster ride" as there are days when the news and emotions are high and others when the news and emotions are low. Yes, there are undramatic adoptions, but the prospective adoptive family should be prepared for the drama and roller coaster of emotions during this period. Attention to detail, frequent communication, and excellence in the delivery of professional services to the birth parents may go a long way to reduce the drama, but no matter what level of service is provided, anything can happen.

Obviously, the duration of the waiting period is based on the dates when the match is made and the date when the birth mother delivers. Some women begin the adoption process immediately upon learning of their pregnancy, and others begin after they complete the decision-making process and conclude that adoption is in the best interests of the child as well as themselves. Whatever the time period is, it seems to last forever for both the birth parent(s) and the prospective adoptive family.

During this waiting period, the family should expect the agency to provide them with medical reports of each visit to the OB or any other health-care provider and the family is encouraged to take such reports to their personal physician for an independent and impartial review. The reports will, of course, be redacted to remove the birth mother's name to maintain her privacy and confidentiality.

When the birth mother is being compliant and going to all of her doctor, laboratory, ultrasound, and other appointments, the process appears to be efficient and perhaps the stress level is more manageable.

It is not uncommon for birth parents to have doubts about completing their adoption plan. It's important that the agency or attorney keep in regular touch with the birth parents to understand and work through the issues.

CAUTION

But when one or more appointments are missed or a birth mother falls off the agency's radar for a few days, everyone gets nervous, anxious, and upset about the progress of the adoption. In many cases, the communication gap is caused by a lost cell phone, a family emergency, or an arrest. Whatever the case, it is further support of the fact that adoptions are riddled with stress, anxiety, and drama.

From the perspective of the agency or attorney, we feel that there is no good excuse for a birth mother to fall out of touch. If she lost her cell phone, there's always a way to call, especially since many agencies and attorneys have toll-free numbers. Further, if she's in jail, jails permit inmates to use the telephone service. The absence of communication from the birth mother is disrespectful to the family who's paying her bills and to the professionals who are jumping through hoops to procure services which she needs and would otherwise never be able to receive. Further, it's frustrating to everyone involved and could be symptomatic of a larger problem and should be addressed promptly.

Aside from the all-important medical visits which are scheduled during the waiting period, there's a lot more going on. The birth mother may be working with the agency to get a birth certificate for a state identification card so she can qualify for Medicaid or one of several other assistance programs. There may be Medicaid appointments, counseling sessions, meetings with the family and the agency together, meetings with the agency without the family and any combination thereof.

It is important that the family be kept abreast of all events other than those which are of minor significance. They should know of any equivocation by the birth parent(s) so they can open up a discussion with the agency about what steps should be taken to discover if the equivocation is a product of outside and uninformed influences, if that is the case, or whether the birth parent(s) have reservations about completing the adoption plan. It is not uncommon for birth parents to have doubts about completing their adoption plan. Frequent interaction between the agency and the birth parents will often uncover this equivocation or uncertainty and enable the social worker on the case to immediately address the issues directly with all concerned.

During the waiting period it is important that there be a clear and readily available line of communication open between the birth parent(s) and the agency or attorney. In our agency, the birth parent(s) know they can reach one of the two attorneys on a 24/7 basis because we give them our cell phone numbers and our office telephone system forwards incoming calls to our cell phones after usual business hours. We make it clear to them that we are the attorneys for the agency, and not *their* attorneys, and if they want their own counsel, it is available to them. In the absence of them having their own counsel, we are happy to talk with them about anything they like, so long as they know that we don't represent them.

If a birth mother has an issue at 9 PM, long after the office closes, we would rather she call us to discuss the problem than be troubled by it until the office opens the next day or after the weekend is over. That an agency or attorney is so readily available to birth parents is a reflection of the fact that whatever their issues are, someone cares about them and wants to address them promptly. We think it demonstrates the importance of the adoption process and, of course, specifically the importance of the birth mother in the process. It is also a factor in enabling the birth mother to feel that she is cared for and her needs are respected, because indeed she is and indeed they are.

During the waiting period, it is also important that the prospective adoptive family have access to the adoption professionals with whom they are working. While there is rarely a need to contact the agency or attorney after hours, access to professionals for questions, discussions and explanations should be readily and easily available. Email goes a long way in making it easier for the agency and family to communicate rapidly and frequently. Of course the family should never hesitate to request a face-to-face meeting to discuss any phase of the adoption process given the importance of the event and the emotional and financial commitment by the family.

CAUTION A great meeting between the birth parents and the adoptive family early on is no guarantee whatsoever that the birth mother is not perpetrating a fraud on the family and is not simply gaming the systems for a few month's rent and expenses.

If there is going to be a prebirth meeting with the birth parents, the prospective adoptive family, and the agency or attorney, it will usually take place during the waiting period. Unlike some other adoption entities, we do not do the "dog and pony show" wherein multiple families are trucked in front of the birth parents and the birth parents are expected to choose. Such meetings typically take place over lunch or dinner, and every effort is made to make the meeting as productive as possible giving each of the parties the chance to get to know the other and each will have the chance to ask questions of the other and hopefully get answers. Both the prospective adoptive family and the birth parents are asked to make a list of questions they want to ask and topics they would like to explore so the meeting will be as organized and productive as possible. The meeting is generally more about the birth parent(s) meeting the family than the other way around. Whoever from the agency attends the meeting is expected to keep to an informal agenda and move things along at an acceptable pace. The goal is, of course, to be sure that all reasonable inquiries by each side have been asked and answered within the boundaries of maintaining the privacy and confidentiality of all concerned. We typically do this over a lunch or dinner when all participants can relax and let the agency representative create a beginning, a middle, and an ending to the meeting in as casual and relaxed a manner as practical.

The actual meeting may involve the birth parent(s) bringing some, all, or none of their other children with them, and it is not unusual for a birth mother who has no children and doesn't want to bring the birth father to bring a close relative or friend for moral support. It is especially nice when the birth parents bring another child with them as prospective adoptive families like to see what the baby might look like, even though it is possible that there will be different birth fathers.

We always encourage a birth mother to bring a supportive party with her to the meeting because to attend alone and be confronted with an excited family can be intimidating and sometimes overwhelming, particularly for someone who is not used to this kind of interaction. The goal of these meetings is to have everyone relaxed, comfortable, and easygoing, which is really the best way to have the meeting be productive. No matter how much effort is put into making the parties relaxed, at the outset there is almost always a level of anxiety which subsides as the meeting progresses. The meetings usually take about two hours and hopefully result in each of the parties feeling good about the other and having a higher level of confidence in the outcome of the adoption process. We especially appreciate it when the meeting is over and the parties hug each other. While it guarantees nothing, it is a good sign and we are always looking for good signs.

Our experience is that having already gotten to know each other makes the events which take place at the time of and shortly after the baby is born much easier for the birth parent(s) as they have a good idea as to the type of family that will be raising the child and can now put a face to a name. They will have had the opportunity to ask their questions, in person, and observe the personalities. They will get a peek into the interpersonal chemistry, the sense of harmony, and other characteristics of the people who will be parenting the child. It takes much of the mystery out of the adoption process and makes completing the adoption easier and more emotionally rewarding for the birth parent(s).

On the subject of fraud, we have found that having a great meeting early on in the process is no guarantee whatsoever that the birth mother is not perpetrating a fraud on the family. As previously stated, the women who engage in adoption fraud in an organized and methodical fashion are soulless, and meeting with the family, hearing about their prior losses in their own efforts to deliver a child naturally, hearing their excitement, seeing the pictures of the extended family who are excited about the imminent arrival of the new baby – all of those things are meaningless to the sociopath who is simply leading them on for a few months' rent and expenses.

From the prospective adoptive family's vantage, the meeting is an opportunity to see, in person, at least half of the gene pool from which the child will be born as well as the personality, attitude, sense of humor, concerns, and other aspects of at least one of the birth parents and that will help the family give the child, if and when appropriate, some insight into his or her biological parents.

CHAPTER

12

The Birth of the Child

Without a doubt, the most anxious time for the family is the time when the birth mother is in the hospital just about to or just having given birth. This is the time when there is a convergence of anxiety, relief, happiness, sadness, and many more emotions. There are a number of people involved at this particular time. They include, in addition to the birth parent(s) and the prospective adoptive family, the hospital's case manager and/or social worker, friends and family of the birth parent(s), and, on occasion, a representative from the state's child welfare agency. This is in addition to the nursing staff taking care of the birth mother and the baby's nurses in the newborn nursery or the newborn intensive care unit.

Our experience is that most of the various interested parties are supportive of the birth parent(s)' adoption plans but occasionally there will be people with a different agenda attempting to derail the adoption process that has been evolving and nurtured for so many months during the pregnancy by so many people with so much care and concern.

As do all patients in a health-care facility, birth mothers are medical patients who have rights. They have rights in the hospital, in the obstetrician's office, in the laboratory, and wherever else they are treated. Some of these rights are codified legal rights, and some are moral and ethical rights. These rights include the right not to be belittled or to have their highly personal adoption decision challenged, questioned, or doubted. They have the right not to be badgered into or out of their adoption decision. They have the right to privacy and confidentiality at all phases of the pregnancy as well as during labor, delivery, and recovery. The birth mother has the right to choose, subject to hospital protocol, who she wants present in the delivery room and, of equal importance, who she does not want to participate in any aspect of her delivery or her stay in the hospital.

So, for example, if consistent with hospital protocol, the birth mother can request that a prospective adoptive parent be present in the delivery room. In such event, it will usually be the prospective adoptive mother invited while her husband impatiently waits outside the delivery room. Similarly, if a party such as the birth father (or a member of his family) is not welcome, the birth mother has every right to ask security to remove him from the hospital grounds. This type of situation usually ends up being quite ugly and often ends up involving the police.

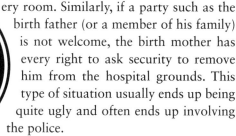

The birth mother has the legal right to decide who can and cannot be present in the delivery room. She is under no obligation to allow any member of the adoptive family to witness the birth.

While in the hospital, it is common procedure for a birth mother to be visited by a hospital social worker/case manager to discuss, in general terms, her adoption plan. It is appropriate for the social worker/case manager to inquire as to whether the birth mother has made her decision voluntarily and free from any external influence or if there was any undue pressure exerted on her to proceed with an adoption. It is acceptable for the caseworker to review community resources available to the birth mother, but it is *not* acceptable for the case worker to pressure the birth mother one way or the other regarding her adoption decision. Social worker/case manager interactions are not to deliver personal opinions, personal feelings, or religious implications to the patient.

It is inappropriate, and in some cases illegal, for a hospital worker to express a personal opinion about the birth mother's decision to complete an adoption plan. The social worker/case manager, nurse, or other person has little or no idea what life events and experiences were considered in the birth mother's decision to place the baby for adoption, and he/she should not interject personal views or opinions. The social worker/case manager has only had a visit or two with the birth mother while in the hospital and thus is in no position to understand the underpinnings of the adoption decision.

There have been a handful of cases in which we have been involved where a social worker/case manager has attempted to interject personal feelings about the subject of adoption. The vast majority of hospital employees and professionals realize what is at stake for the baby, the prospective adoptive family, and the birth parents and honor the rules dealing with nonintervention in such cases. The Florida version can be found in the Florida Statutes at § 383.3105, Patients Consenting to Adoptions; Protocols.

If you are planning to adopt a baby, we *urge* you to find out what, if any, prohibition your state makes against hospital workers counseling birth mothers into or out of placing their babies for adoption, and carry a printout of that regulation with you when you visit the hospital, *just in case*. The Florida version can be found in the appendix to this tome.

We have, however, experienced a few situations where, because of personal or religious beliefs, hospital staff members berated birth mothers for their decision to do what they believed was best for their babies. One experience involved a hospital social worker, who had herself been unable to achieve a pregnancy and had one or more unsuccessful adoption attempts, who attempted to dissuade a birth mother from completing her adoption plan by making bizarre statements. She made other unprofessional and inappropriate statements in an attempt to influence the birth mother to choose a different course of action for herself and the baby. This type of behavior is usually engaged in by people who have no idea what the birth parents' motivation is for placing a baby for adoption or simply have a religious or other critical view of adoption which is, at best, misdirected. It is completely unacceptable. In this particular case, the social worker had suffered pregnancy-related losses and had taken it upon herself to make sure that if she couldn't adopt a baby, no one could. Due to this and other similar occurrences, she was eventually removed from her duties in the maternity section of the health-care facility and then ultimately fired.

Securing the Consent to Adopt from Birth Parent(s)

As previously noted, each state has unique laws, rules, and regulations governing just about every aspect of adoption. Securing the legal and binding consent document from the birth parent(s) of the child is one of the most important steps in the adoption process, and it must be accomplished in strict compliance with the applicable state's laws. Most importantly, the birth parent(s)'s consent must be given knowingly, intelligently, and voluntarily and in the absence of fraud or duress.

We are not going to discuss the variety of state regulatory patterns which govern this area other than to use Florida as an example of just one state's legal requirements for the consent process. From this discussion, we think you will get the sense of importance of this aspect of the process.

In Florida, a birth father may execute an Affidavit of Nonpaternity which is the equivalent of a legally binding consent to adopt. This instrument may be executed before the birth of the baby. It must be signed in the presence of two witnesses (who may be of his choosing) and a notary public. Once signed, this document is irrevocable unless it was secured by fraud or duress.

A birth mother, on the other hand, may not sign a legally binding consent to adoption until after the baby is born. Her consent must also be witnessed and notarized as above. The timing of the birth mother's consent signing is important and is dictated by state law.

Each state has prescribed time periods during which such consents may be signed. By way of example, Florida law permits the birth mother to execute a consent to adoption at the earlier of 48 hours after the birth of the child or the day on which she is notified in writing of her discharge from the hospital. Therefore, if the birth mother has a C-section, consent papers may not be signed until 48 hours after the baby is born even if the birth mother wants to do so earlier or leaves the hospital in less than 48 hours against medical advice. The consent may be signed after 48 hours even if the birth mother remains in the hospital. If the birth mother has a vaginal delivery and the physician determines that she is fit to be discharged the day after the delivery (which happens more often than not), the birth mother can consent on the day she is notified in writing (via a note to her patient chart, for example) that she has been discharged.

In any event, whether the consent is signed on the day of discharge or after the passage of 48 hours after birth, the consent under Florida law is irrevocable unless obtained by fraud or duress. Many states, however, have laws permitting a birth parent to revoke a consent within a prescribed number of days for any reason or for no reason. This, of course, presents a major anxiety issue in the lives of the adoptive family as they will likely be bonding with and caring for the baby while hoping no revocation takes place. In our opinion, it is brutal and unwarranted to provide a postconsent revocation period to the birth parent(s).

In addition to the required witnesses and notary public, it is prudent, but not required by law, to have a court reporter present to memorialize the event, word by word, to assist in avoiding a subsequent dispute over what actually occurred at the consent execution proceeding. For adoptions of newborns, the consent signing process typically takes place in the hospital and those present include the birth mother, the birth father, two witnesses, a notary public, a court reporter, and the attorney for the agency. There can be more people present and possibly less if, for example, the court reporter is also a notary public.

At the consent signing, in addition to the obvious questions about the identification of who is signing papers, we feel it's important to document

We were contacted by a couple who reported to us that they were "hiding out" in an undisclosed location, somewhere within the State of Florida. They had adopted a baby in California one month prior, had taken the baby home to their home – State of Virginia – and were patiently awaiting the finalization of the adoption when the birth mother called the adoption lawyer and advised that due to family pressures she wanted her baby back. California is one of those states with a revocation provision in its adoption laws, and the birth mother was well within her rights to cancel the adoption at that point.

The couple advised that they had come to Florida because they knew that birth mothers in Florida could not revoke their adoption consents (absent fraud/duress), so they thought that being in Florida would offer them some type of advantage in the case. Unfortunately for them, however, the adoption was a California adoption and even if they were Florida residents, Florida law would not have any application to the adoption proceedings in California. In fact, they had bigger issues, in that they had left California without ICPC approval, and were essentially "hiding out" with someone else's baby, possibly invoking the criminal laws of kidnapping and/or false imprisonment!

Ultimately, this couple traveled back to California and handed the baby over to the birth mother's attorney, as legally required.

that the birth mother has taken no pain or other medication or consumed any substance which would in any way alter her ability to think clearly. We ask the birth mother what she perceives the consent-taking process is designed to accomplish. Additionally, we want to be sure she knows the difference between foster care and adoption and that the consent she is giving is for adoption (permanent) and not foster care (temporary).

CAUTION

Many states permit a birth parent to revoke a consent to adoption within a prescribed number of days for any reason or for no reason at all. Understandably, this can create enormous anxiety in the adoptive family.

We also make inquiry into whether she is signing papers voluntarily and then ask for her definition of the word "voluntarily." We also want to be sure that she understands that, in effect, once the consent papers are signed they are irrevocable and we ask her to articulate her understanding of the word "irrevocable." We then of course qualify this by advising her that her "consent" was never actually given if she is able to prove in a court of law that she was coerced or defrauded into signing the consent papers. At the time consents are taken, birth parents are again advised of their right to have independent representation by an attorney who has no affiliation with the agency and that such attorney will be provided at no expense to the birth parent(s).

Other areas of inquiry during this transcribed consent-signing event include an inquiry into the identification of the birth father of the child and whether any man has financially or emotionally supported the birth mother during the pregnancy and/or after the birth of the child. We ask whether the birth mother is married or was ever married and whether she is or has lived with a man at any time within the past year in order to ascertain if any other consent to the adoption is required. While at this point of the process we already know the answers to those questions, it is important ask them on the record because during this process the birth mother is under oath and has sworn to tell the truth at the risk of committing perjury whereas in all prior conversations with the birth mother she was not under oath and there were no consequences for her failure to be truthful.

We think it is also important to ask the birth mother whether anyone has offered her anything of value to sign the consent papers. This is done, obviously, to eliminate any possible suggestion of inappropriate conduct by the agency or its attorneys to secure the consent. Another formality we engage in is asking the birth parents whether they were treated with respect and dignity throughout the process by the agency and its attorneys to counter any subsequent allegation of inappropriate behavior toward them. This technique is available to defend against any allegation of disrespectful or inappropriate conduct by the agency to secure the consent.

When taking the consent, it is important to confirm with the birth parents that each of the documents they are being asked to sign has been reviewed by and explained to them word by word and that they understand the documents and have no unanswered questions.

The foundation for all of this attention and perhaps overemphasis on detail is that we don't want a birth parent to sign a consent unless he or she fully understands the consequences and fully intends to place the child for adoption. This is especially true of what is known as the Adoption Disclosure form which is basically the equivalent of the bible of adoption rights.

The family is never present for this procedure because having to state the birth parents names as well as the family's names for the court reporter would defeat the concept of privacy and confidentiality of the entire adoption process. That said, and as an aside, is very likely that the prospective adoptive family will learn the last name of the birth mother because of the information that they are exposed to in the nursery; however, the birth mother has no such way of learning the names of the prospective adoptive family and that level of confidentiality is critical.

We are frequently asked what constitutes fraud and duress to cause a consent to be revocable. Here are a few examples:

- If one were to promise to provide postdelivery living expenses to a birth mother for rent, food, utilities, counseling, and other permissible reasonable and necessary living expenses and one were to fail to do so, one may have defrauded her.
- If birth parents require and the agency/attorney represents a specific family dynamic for the adoptive family (single, married, kids, no kids, married for a certain number of years, specific ethnicity, sexual orientation, specific religion, etc.) and the agency/attorney places the baby with an adoptive family outside of those parameters, the consent may well be revocable based on fraud for failure to adhere to the requirements of the birth parents.
- If the agency/attorney misrepresents the background information on the prospective adoptive family (such as their marital status, educational background, health, legal status, or other important background issue), the consents may be revocable based on fraudulent misrepresentations.
- If a birth mother is on probation for a criminal offense and a condition of that probation is her cessation of drug use and the agency/attorney has a laboratory test showing a positive result for illegal drug use during the pregnancy and suggests that the laboratory test will be provided to a probation officer if the birth mother doesn't sign the consent, the consent is likely revocable based on it having been procured under duress.

The circumstances giving rise to fraud or duress are limited only by one's imagination. Such activities should never be engaged in by any ethical or responsible adoption professional.

Once the birth parent's consent is signed, a copy is provided to the birth parent(s) and a copy of the birth mother's consent is attached to the baby's chart in the nursery so the hospital staff will know that there is an adoption in process for the baby, the identity of the agency or attorney responsible for the adoption, and the identity of the child's legal guardian. In Florida, once the consent is executed, the agency becomes the legal guardian of the baby and is to be treated by the hospital the same way the hospital would treat the biological mother of the baby.

CHAPTER

14

After Delivery and Consent but Before the Birth Mother Is Discharged from the Hospital

After the birth of the child and after the required consent papers are signed but prior to her discharge from the hospital, the birth mother of the baby can spend time with the baby if permitted to do so by the legal guardian. This assumes that there is no legal prohibition against the birth mother having such contact with the baby. It would be highly unusual for visitations to be denied to the birth mother absent some compelling reason, such as a history of violence against children or that she and/or the baby are currently suffering from drug withdrawal. This is usually about the birth mother saying good-bye to the baby, and it is often, as you can imagine, highly emotional.

It is also typical for birth parent(s) to decide that since they are not going to parent the child, they choose not to spend any significant time with the baby. However, if the birth parents do want to spend time with the baby, the agency or attorney should arrange for them to have that opportunity while the baby remains in the nursery.

There are several variables of the "after birth but before birth mother discharge" scenario. The birth parent(s) can elect to have the baby in the room with them for some alone time enabling them to have some private moments to say good-bye to the child alone or perhaps with only certain family or friends present. The birth parent(s) may decide to share their predischarge time with the adoptive family so they can observe and enjoy the initial contact and interaction between the baby and the adoptive parents. The birth parent(s) may not want to see the baby at all deciding that it might be too emotional and too difficult for them given the fact that they have chosen to place the baby for adoption. It could also be that the

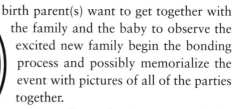

The contrast of emotions between the birth parent(s) saying good-bye to the child and the adoptive parents taking the baby home is poignant for everyone involved in the adoption.

birth parent(s) want to get together with the family and the baby to observe the excited new family begin the bonding process and possibly memorialize the event with pictures of all of the parties together.

Regardless of what approach the birth parent(s) take, the emotions in the room have the potential to be dramatic in that the birth parent(s) may well experience some sense of loss (or relief) and the adoptive family will be on cloud nine with excitement, anxiety, a mix of appreciation for what the birth parents did, and a sense of sorrow that the birth parent(s) found themselves in the situation that created this moment.

From our perspective as adoption professionals, the time the birth mother spends with the baby has its positives and negatives. We are happy to see the birth mother taking the opportunity to give herself whatever closure she needs in seeing the baby off to his or her new life, and honored by the trust she has for the decisions we've made for the baby, as we often are the ones who made the choice of the new family via the match. However, we've got the nursery asking us when the baby's going home, the adoptive family jumping out of their skin to leave the hospital and take the baby home, and the office calling, asking when we're going to be back, because we've got 400 messages to return. Therefore, from a practical perspective, it's somewhat of a burden to spend the day in the hospital if the mother is delaying handing over the reins, so to speak.

If the baby is in the regular newborn nursery, visiting arrangements are made quite easily and the baby may well spend time in the room with the birth parent(s) (and the adoptive family) for much of the hospital stay, thus making visiting, feeding, changing, and caring for the baby relatively convenient.

If the baby is in the newborn intensive care unit (NICU), the baby will not be able to leave that unit until a pediatrician determines that the baby is ready to step down in the level of care to the regular newborn nursery until eventually discharged from the hospital. There are many reasons the baby is placed in the NICU including, among others, premature birth, low birth weight, undeveloped respiratory system, inability to bottle feed thus necessitating a feeding tube, infection, and, among others, the baby's withdrawal from drugs taken by the birth mother during the pregnancy. Whatever the case may be, the baby will be closely monitored in the NICU and the prospective adoptive family will be able to visit in accordance with NICU policy and learn about the very specific care needed for the baby.

Once adoption consent papers are signed, it is customary for the prospective adoptive family to have the same level of access to the NICU as the birth mother would have. The duration of a baby's stay in the NICU is a function of the condition giving rise to the confinement. During their visits with the baby in the NICU, the adoptive family will have access to the specific nurses caring for the baby as well as the pediatricians directing the medical treatment. While having a child in the NICU is difficult for a new parent, on the positive side, it is a good time to get educated on the child's condition and any future actions which may be required to treat the child after discharge from hospital.

One of the most difficult experiences a family will have occurs when the baby is in the NICU withdrawing from a drug used by the birth mother during the pregnancy. Withdrawal episodes are difficult to witness. It is painful for the baby, and it is painful for the adoptive parents who are at least capable of understanding the reasons for such episodes. The baby is the one who truly suffers and is the one who had no role in creating this situation.

A family should seek out as much knowledge and understanding as they can on the specific drug from which the baby is withdrawing to learn about the after effects of the drug, if any, on the baby's development.

Studies are constantly being performed on the progress of children who were exposed to drugs during pregnancy to see the levels of progress made as the children grow older. Much of the literature is encouraging, but a thorough understanding of the specific situation is required.

At some point prior to a birth mother's discharge from the hospital, the in-house birth certificate office representative will visit her and request that she complete the forms necessary to enable the state to issue a birth certificate for the newborn baby. She can name the baby on the birth certificate or not – the decision is hers. She will probably already have been told that the prospective adoptive family will certainly choose a new name for the baby and that at some point a new birth certificate will be issued in the name chosen by the prospective adoptive family after the adoption is finalized.

It is also at this time that the birth mother has to make a decision as to whether to identify the father of the child on the birth certificate if she is not legally married. In the case of a married birth mother, the husband's name will appear on the birth certificate even if the husband (the "legal father") is not the birth (biological) father. Our experience is that the large majority of the unmarried women with whom we work choose not to identify a birth father on the birth certificate questionnaire. Further, most birth mothers choose to name the baby understanding that the first, middle, and last names will almost certainly be changed.

Discharge of Baby from Hospital

Babies with no significant medical issues are customarily discharged from the hospital between two and four days after birth. Babies in the NICU are generally discharged when the condition which placed them there appears to have been treated and resolved, fully or partially, to the point where the attending pediatrician believes that the child will be best served completing his recovery at home with the family. Babies who are born prematurely are usually expected to stay in the nursery or NICU for the length of time it would take for them to have been full-term. However, this rule of thumb appears to be the exception, not the rule. We have never seen a baby stay in the NICU for the full amount of time between the birth and the due date, absent other considerations such as opiate addition. There is of course no predetermined time for the cessation of care in either nursery – it all depends on the baby's health and ability to successfully respond to treatment.

Whenever it is that the discharge does occur, it is usually a stressful, happy, sad, and special event. It is customary for the nursing staff to have a training session with the adoptive parents shortly before discharge in which they discuss feeding, correct sleeping and napping positions, diaper changing, treatment of the umbilical cord, taking the baby's temperature, properly reacting to out-of-range baby temperature, determining when it is appropriate to call either 911 or a doctor discussing the need for training in infant CPR, among others, and how to dress the baby insofar as the proper number of layers of clothing for the climate in which the baby lives.

Prior to the nursery's training session with the new parents, we advise them to listen carefully, ask any questions they have, but that the session is not an opportunity to have a long personal conversation with the nurses about how your sister is a nurse and she told you to do it the other way. The nurses have to get back to work, we want to scram from the hospital as soon as possible, and theories and processes change over time. Great, you laid your other kids on their side to sleep, but now the recommended position is on the back. We're certain that this fact shouldn't precipitate a 25-minute monologue about how your grandmother used to do it!

A printed summary of the baby's stay in the nursery or NICU from admission to discharge will often be provided to the legal guardian. This will usually include the results of a hearing test, immunization shots given, and will indicate that a metabolic screening test was done to identify any harmful or potentially serious disorders that were not apparent at the time of birth, including those which can interfere with or prevent an infant's normal physical or mental development. The metabolic screening assists in identifying any problems at an early stage and can make a huge difference in the treatment of such disorders and possibly enable the baby to avoid permanent interference with a healthy development. The metabolic screening test typically involves only a drop of blood taken from the baby's heel at about 48 hours of age. The blood sample is sent to a laboratory for evaluation, and the results are given to the legal guardian. Test results which indicate one or more specific disorders may be a false-positive, and therefore, the test will typically be redone. The metabolic screening tests are performed on all newborns unless the parents opt out of the non-legally required tests. The screening requirements are determined by each state, and they address approximately 30 disorders, many of which may be inherited from the biological parents.

> **NOTE**
>
> State laws generally require that a baby being placed for adoption when discharged from the hospital be released to the care and custody of the legal guardian (oftentimes the adoption agency) or to the adoption attorney. The attorney will then release the child to the adoptive parents outside the hospital.

Another test often done shortly before discharge is the newborn car seat test which takes about 90 to 120 minutes and is usually done in the nursery. The test is generally for premature babies born before 37 weeks of gestation. A premature baby's airways are usually weaker than a full-term baby's airways and may collapse when the baby is placed in a car seat in a semi-reclining position. Thus, the close observation during the car seat test should give assurance that the infant is capable of assuming that physical position with minimal risk.

It is important for new family to be fully trained in the use of any medical device which a baby requires at the time of discharge. For example, a sleep apnea device which monitors a baby's breathing while asleep may be necessary. A baby's breathing can stop and start repeatedly necessitating the use of a monitor to alert parents of an interruption in the breathing. Sleep apnea is more prevalent in babies born prematurely. This condition is addressed in the newborn nursery, and if it persists when the baby is discharged, the apnea monitor is an effective method of reducing the risks of any serious injury to the baby's health. Thus, parents taking home infants with sleep apnea are trained in how to use the monitor to reduce health risks to the baby.

Another of the key components in the discharge process is checking and double checking the wrist and ankle band numbers placed on the baby at the moment of birth against the band numbers on the baby's chart at the time of discharge to be certain that the correct baby is being discharged. It is extremely rare that any such mix-up can occur, and it is easily preventable.

State laws generally require that a baby being placed for adoption when discharged from the hospital be released to the care and custody of the legal guardian (oftentimes the adoption agency) or to the adoption attorney. The simple reason for this is that in the eyes of the law, the adoption agency or adoption attorney to whom consent was issued by the birth parents is the only entity which the court should look to as being responsible for the child. Further, the hospital is not in a position to determine who will or will not be the adoptive family and thus is not required to make any such decisions. It simply must discharge the baby to the legal guardian once a pediatrician determines that the baby is healthy enough to be discharged from the hospital. That said, however, in private attorney adoptions, in Florida, the court may designate the prospective adoptive family as the legal guardians of the child pending finalization or other court action, thus enabling the hospital to discharge the child directly to the parents as opposed to the agency or lawyer.

A gigantic burden is placed, not necessarily voluntarily, on the hospital administrators, staff, social workers, and nurses, by adoption-related proceedings and activities that occur within the hospital. As if they didn't have enough to do already, hospital administrators and policy-writers have to figure out to whom the birth mother's medical information can be given and with whom and in front of whom it can be discussed; how to handle visitors to the baby and information from the baby's chart when the baby is in the NICU or nursery; how, when, where, and to whom a baby can be discharged; whether the state's child protective agency should be alerted in any given situation, such as if the birth mother or baby tests positive for drugs, or the birth mother or any party is acting in such a way as to cause concern or raise red flags. If I, as a lawyer, had to know as much about nursing as they, as nurses, had to know about the law, I would have no patience!

After the nursing staff transports the baby to the hospital's front door, the legal guardian transfers the baby to the adoptive family who will secure the baby in the car seat in the rear seat facing the rear of the car and head for home and what is expected to be a lifetime of parenting.

New parents are encouraged to take the baby to a pediatrician within 48 hours of discharge, and the visit will essentially be the first step in tracking and monitoring the child's medical history. The pediatrician should be given a copy of the discharge summary and all other hospital records which the family receives from the legal guardian at the time of discharge in order to begin the baby's new health record. Such records will have the birth mother's name redacted to protect her privacy.

Post-discharge Legal Proceedings and Events

Once settled in at home, it is important that the family contact the social worker who issued the family's home study if it is the same person who will be providing follow-up reports on the baby's and the family's progress together. These are called "postplacement reports," and they form the basis for the agency, in its capacity as legal guardian, to issue a written consent to adopt in favor of the adoptive family. Remember, the legal guardian must, after carefully reviewing the postplacement reports, determine whether it is in the child's best interests that the agency consent to the adoption. The court in which the adoption is pending must approve of the agency's consent.

The foundation of this system of making adoptive placements is *trust*. The lawyers must trust the social workers and vice versa. The agency must trust the social workers and vice versa. The court must trust the lawyers and the agency. Let's face it, anyone can put anything they want in a report, it's all very subjective, and writing skills come heavily into play. Two different social workers could observe the same situation and come away with two different impressions of what they just saw.

Most of the judges before whom we've appeared have been intelligent, thoughtful, caring, and have wanted to do what's right by the child. Most of them, at the very least, scan through the various petitions, reports, summaries, and the other volume of paperwork created for any given case. However, it would be a lot to expect every judge to not only read carefully through every report but to take the additional efforts to confirm the information. Therefore, the judges must trust the professionals who have submitted these various filings to have put the work in and to have submitted accurate and well-reasoned reports and recommendations. It's the lawyers who will look like idiots if this was not done correctly, and at the end of the day, our most important and valuable asset is credibility.

During this post-discharge period, while the family is settling into their new lives, the agency and its attorneys will be completing the legal steps to terminate the parental rights of the birth parents and preparing and filing such other documentation as will be necessary to both the termination of parental rights proceeding and the finalization of the adoption which will ultimately make the prospective adoptive family the legal parents of the child and remove the agency from being the child's legal guardian.

It is also possible that, during this time, the birth parent(s) will request some pictures and perhaps an update letter as to the baby's progress. The agency or attorney should facilitate that process. Further, during this period it is common for both the adoptive family and the birth parent(s), separately, to seek counseling to assist them in dealing with the new realities which confront them. There is virtually no way to know the type and extent of counseling which may fit each situation, and thus, the agency must be flexible and be able to be sure counseling is available to the birth parent(s) and the prospective adoptive family as and when needed.

As a general proposition, counseling does not do anything but waste time and money when it is forced upon a party. Some agencies and lawyers "require" birth mothers to go to certain types of counseling to discuss their adoption-related feelings, even though some birth mothers would simply rather not. There is probably an element of liability mitigation to this requirement – if something untoward happens with the birth mother during or after the adoption process, the agency will be able to say that the birth mother received counseling – but the value of such a requirement is dubious at best. We make counseling very available and attractive, and we hope that the birth mothers will take advantage of it for their own benefit, but we do not "require" mandatory attendance at counseling sessions. Our experience is that the majority of birth parents do not seek post-delivery counseling.

Finalizing the Adoption

Although the details of each state's adoption laws are different, there are common threads which run through all of such laws and the discussion below of the legal process, while general in nature, pretty well tracks the important legal steps.

Once the family is matched with birth parents and all of the necessary preliminary paperwork is signed by the birth parent(s) and the binding paperwork is signed by the prospective adoptive family establishing its relationship with the adoption agency or the adoption attorney, the agency's attorneys will typically file a confidential petition in court to provide and clarify the details and the general parameters of the proposed adoption, including amounts of financial assistance projected to be provided to the birth mother.

There are a variety of different approaches for how the states address the concepts and philosophies surrounding birth mother expenses. For example, some states do not allow for prenatal expenses to be paid during an adoption plan. Other states, such as Florida, allow for an adoptive family, through their agency or lawyer, to pay for a certain minimal amount of expenses without a court order. The court must order expenses that exceed that maximum. So long as the items in the Petition appear reasonable, the Court is likely to sign the order allowing for the additional support.

Unscrupulous lawyers have been known to take advantage of the adoption situation by misreporting or failing altogether to report monies spent for expenses. If your lawyer or agency is paying for limo rides to and from nail salons for the birth mother, you may inadvertently be participating in a felony called "baby selling." Nail salons, limo rides, and spa treatments are NOT reasonable and necessary, as contemplated by the law.

One of the reasons that average families cannot afford to adopt babies through private agencies and lawyers is that these activities take place, thus driving up not only the costs of adoption but the expectation of the birth mothers. Now, when that birth mother has a friend who is pregnant, you can bet your bottom dollar she'll say "call the lawyer who helped me, she'll send you by limo to nail salons and day spas!" You can also safely assume that there will be some kind of commission or finder's fee paid to the referring friend, again likely contrary to law. Shame on them!

What Happens in Court

An initial petition will be filed in court to commence the adoption case. The agency's attorneys will then seek to secure a court order permitting the adoption to proceed and to place the child with the prospective adoptive family once the required consents of the birth parent(s) are secured and all other state law prerequisites have been met. The court may also approve of the use of the family's funds to pay birth mother medical and reasonable and necessary living expenses as well as court and other appropriate costs and the agency or attorney's fees.

After the birth of the child, the next important step in the court process is filing the petition to terminate the parental rights of the birth mother and the birth father, whether he is identified or not and whether he is known or not. This legal proceeding to terminate the parental rights of the birth parents is possibly the most important court proceeding in the adoption process. The petition should be filed as soon after the birth mother signs the consent to the adoption as possible.

The petition for termination of parental rights will essentially ask the court for a judgment terminating the parental rights of the birth mother based on the fact that she knowingly, intelligently, and voluntarily executed a consent to adoption (filed as an exhibit to the petition) and that all requirements of the state law have been met. The petitioner will ask the court to terminate the parental rights of the birth father because he (i) signed a consent to the adoption (or its equivalent); (ii) in the case of an unmarried birth mother who cannot or refuses to identify the birth father, he has not filed a claim of paternity with the state and there is no way to know who or where he is; (iii) in the case of a known but unlocatable birth father, a diligent search for his whereabouts was conducted and did not yield his address and he was not registered in a putative father registry; (iv) in the case of a known and locatable birth father, he was personally served with a notice that a court hearing will be held at a given time and location and that his failure to appear either personally or through counsel may result in a default against him, eliminating

> **NOTE**
>
> The legal proceeding to terminate the parental rights of the birth parents is possibly the most important court proceeding in the adoption process. The petition should be filed as soon after the birth mother signs the consent to the adoption as possible.

the necessity for his consent to the adoption; or (v) in the case of a married birth mother, her husband has either executed a consent to the adoption, (or its equivalent), or, if he cannot be located after a diligent search is made, he is notified of the court hearing to terminate his parental rights by publication, thus causing him to be in default enabling the court to terminate his parental rights if he fails to appear in court personally or through counsel.

Many adoptions in our agency have an unknown birth father or the birth mother refuses to identify him and a search of the putative father registry reflects that no claim of paternity has been filed for the child. Thus, in many cases the birth father's consent is not required.

If the attorney engaged a court reporter to document the consent signing proceeding, the transcript should be filed with the court to reflect the fact that, in the best case scenario, the birth mother (i) was reminded of her right to have her own independent counsel; (ii) was questioned about any pain medication or other substance she may have taken before the consent was signed (it's a good idea to ask the birth mother and the nursing staff to refrain from making such pain medication available for at least four hours before signing); (iii) was asked whether she was signing the legal documents at that moment knowingly, willingly, voluntarily, and irrevocably and whether she understood those terms; (iv) was asked whether she was given anything of value to induce her to sign the papers; (v) was asked whether she and the attorney reviewed word by word the papers she was about to sign; (vi) was asked if she understood that once signed, the consent is irrevocable absent fraud or duress (under Florida law); (vii) was asked the identity of the father of the baby and whether or not he provided her with any meaningful emotional or financial assistance during the pregnancy or subsequent thereto; (viii) was asked if she would describe the difference between foster care and adoption and if she understood that the process she was involved in was an adoption; (ix) was asked if she is married or is living with a man; and (x) was asked whether she wants to have independent counsel which would be provided at no cost to her. We also confirm that the birth parent(s) read and understand the documentation, and we inquire about their desire to ask questions about the process. There are, of course, other areas and issues during this proceeding, but these are the main matters to be covered.

Termination of Parental Rights

A court proceeding to terminate parental rights is the legal step taken to end the parent–child relationship and open the door to the finalization of an adoption, thus making the adoptee the legal child of the adoptive family. Of course this step is taken in furtherance of securing the stability, security, safety, and permanency of a forever family for the child.

Every state has a law that dictates the process necessary to accomplish the termination of parental rights, whether the rights are terminated voluntarily or involuntarily.

An involuntary termination of parental rights is initiated by the state and involves proving in court that there is clear and convincing evidence that the parent whose rights are being terminated has abused, neglected, or abandoned the child pre- or postbirth and is thus deemed unfit to be a parent. If it is determined that the child's best interests would be best served by a termination of parental rights, a court will enter an order to do so.

If there are questions of abuse, neglect, or abandonment surrounding the conduct of the child's parents, it is important, before parental rights are terminated involuntarily, that the court know (i) what type of abuse existed (emotional, physical, sexual), (ii) how the child was neglected (instability in living and eating conditions, failure to communicate with or have contact with the child), or (iii) whether the child was abandoned (left to fend for himself or herself with no parental assistance). Drug and alcohol abuse are two of the leading factors which give rise to circumstances which eventually serve as grounds for the finding of abuse, neglect, or abandonment as is mental illness.

If the state cannot identify family members who are willing and able to care for a child and any planned attempt to reunify the child with a parent has failed, a court will likely find sufficient grounds to terminate parental rights and the child then will be available for adoption.

NOTE

In Florida and in many other states, a consent signed under oath and in the presence of two witnesses and a notary public may not be revoked by the birth parent signing unless the parent was defrauded or coerced into signing.

As with most other aspects of adoption, the grounds for termination of parental rights vary from state to state, but the ultimate goal of doing what's in the best interests of the child is the common thread running through every state's laws.

It is also possible in many states to terminate parental rights of a person who has been convicted of a sexual offense or other crimes and has been sentenced to serve time in prison.

There are other grounds for a court to involuntarily terminate parental rights. Such other grounds include the following:

- Failure to support a child
- Failure to maintain contact with a child
- A determination that returning the child to the home of the birth parents would place the child in an at-risk situation.
- The inability to locate a known birth father who has failed to take steps required to protect and assert any parental rights he may have to the child.
- The child was conceived as a result of rape or incest.
- The identity of the birth father is unknown and, whoever he is, he has not provided the child with either or both financial and emotional support.

There are other grounds for an involuntary termination of parental rights, but the above represent the most frequently used grounds in our experience.

Most adoptions are based on the voluntarily relinquishment of the child by the birth mother and, occasionally, the birth father. The birth mother typically executes a legally binding consent to the adoption, thus permitting the adoption agency to take the next step and petition the court for a judgment terminating her parental rights based on the voluntary actions she has taken.

Once the consent is signed and any statutory revocation period expires, a hearing will be held to examine the facts supporting the request for a termination of parental rights and if the grounds have been met, a judge will sign such an order opening the door to the finalization of the adoption.

As mentioned earlier, each state has different procedures which must be followed. In Florida, a consent signed under oath and in the presence of two witnesses and a notary public may not be revoked by the birth parent signing unless the parent was defrauded or coerced into signing. If there is no fraud or duress, the consent is irrevocable immediately upon its execution. If there is fraud or duress and it is so proven in a court of law, the consent was never freely given and thus may be revoked if the attempt to revoke is filed within one year of the date the court enters a judgment terminating parental rights.

An unmarried birth father's parental rights can be terminated based on his signing the equivalent of consent documents or due to his not being known to the birth mother and thus not identifiable. The birth mother may also refuse to identify the birth father (she has the right to privacy) for her own reasons (i.e., she may be afraid of him or, if he is married or in another relationship, she may not want to interfere with it). If a birth father is identified and located and served with appropriate court papers offering him the opportunity to come to court to assert any parental rights he may have and explain why it is not in the child's best interest to have his rights terminated and he fails to appear in court either personally or through an attorney, his parental rights may be terminated by default. This method of termination of parental rights of a birth father is common, and our experience suggests that most unmarried birth fathers do not want to parent a baby and frequently disclaim paternity on the grounds of not knowing how many other potential birth fathers there may be and thereby doubting that they are the father of the child.

If grounds for terminating parental rights are not clearly found, a trial will be scheduled for the petitioner to prove its case.

Let there be no doubt that a trial is the most stressful situation for all involved because we are dealing with a human's life – a child who has likely been living with the prospective adoptive family for many months or years under the cloud of uncertainty. Needless to say, this should be avoided if at all possible.

In the typical adoption termination of parental rights case, both parents' rights are sought to be terminated at the same time. If only one parent's parental rights are terminated, the child can remain with the parent whose rights have not been terminated. In such cases, the child will not be deemed available for adoption until there is a resolution of the matter. Many states permit a child to be placed with a prospective adoptive family when only one parent has executed legal consent documents or has had parental rights terminated while the other parent's rights are undetermined. This is considered to be an at-risk adoption, and the at-risk element is removed when both parents' parental rights have been terminated.

Some states have statutory provisions permitting the termination of parental rights to take place at the same time as the final hearing of adoption in cases such as relative adoptions or stepparent adoptions, thus streamlining the legal process for the child and for the prospective adoptive family.

Putative Father Registry

A putative father is an unmarried man who is presumed or alleged to be the father of the pregnancy or the child.

A putative father registry is a data bank operated by certain states (approximately 33 states have such a registry) and is maintained for men as an option to voluntarily acknowledge paternity of a child born or to be born to a woman to whom he is not married. The putative father may choose to register himself based on a sexual encounter he had and which may have resulted in a pregnancy. By entering his name in the registry, the putative father protects himself from having his parental rights terminated without his receiving notice and an opportunity to establish that the child's best interest would be served by his parenting the child. In other words, after the sexual encounter, a man has the option to enter his name and other information into a registry in order to assure that he is notified when a court action is taken to terminate parental rights as part of an overall adoption process.

Being in the registry does not guarantee a putative father custody of or any legal rights to the child; rather, it assures him notice of the pending action to terminate parental rights and the right to appear in court to testify about what the putative father believes would be in the child's best interest.

Each state with a registry has a specific time frame during which the man may enter his name in the registry and it ranges from the time the sexual encounter occurred to a specified time after birth (i.e., the date on which a petition to terminate parental rights was filed in court).

Although the information typically required to be provided by a man who voluntarily claims paternity varies from state to state, the following information, in one form or another, may be required:

- Name, address, date of birth, and Social Security number of both the birth mother and the putative father
- A physical description of the father and the mother
- If already born, the child's name, date, and place of birth
- The date and location of conception
- A confirmation that the putative father is willing and intends to support the child
- A notarized and dated signature of the putative father

Florida allows a putative father to designate and identify an agent, such as an attorney, parent, or friend, to receive notice of a termination of parental rights proceeding and/or adoption proceeding and that agent's address and signature must appear on the putative father registry registration form.

After having read that the registration and claim of paternity by the putative father is voluntary, one might ask just how frequently does a man not married to a woman with whom he had a sexual relationship choose to step up to the plate and register. The answer, based on our working with the Florida Putative Father Registry since its formation in June 2003, is *almost never*. In fact, since 2003, we have searched the registry over 750 times and found only one man registered.

At the risk of sounding cynical or insensitive, the reality is that when confronted with the prospect of voluntarily entering their name into the putative father registry and thus potentially being liable for up to 18 years of child support, men almost always choose not to register. In many cases, the man may not be sure that he's the father of the pregnancy and his decision may be based on that lack of certainty.

It bears repeating that the man who enters his name in the registry simply gets notice of termination of parental rights or adoption proceeding. He continues to be responsible for many other statutory obligations toward the birth mother which, if he ignores, may well result in his parental rights being terminated even if he is in the registry. So, for example, being in the registry does not mean that the putative father can fail to support the birth mother during her pregnancy, thus abandoning her and the unborn child and then expect to be awarded custody of the child.

Now that we know what the putative father registry is, how does that work itself into the process for termination of parental rights?

If we do not know who the biological father is because the unmarried birth mother says she does not know his name or how she can find that information or if we don't know the birth father's identity because the birth mother refuses to identify him (which she is legally permitted to do), a search of the putative father registry will tell us that there either is or is not someone claiming paternity of the child and to whom, if anyone, we must give notice of the pending legal actions. If no one is in the registry, the court will typically terminate the parental rights of the unknown birth father or the birth father who the birth mother refused to identify due to his failure to submit his name to the registry and thus be in default eliminating the need for his consent to the adoption.

NOTE

The final court hearing usually is a day of joy and celebration for the adoptive family. At the hearing, the family confirms under oath that they understand their legal rights, duties, and responsibilities with respect to the child being adopted.

In all adoptions, including those with an identified birth father or legal father, even if he signs a Consent to Adoption or an Affidavit of Non-paternity, we think that a search of the putative father registry should be made to determine if anyone has filed a claim of paternity for the born or as-yet-unborn child. If no one appears in the registry, a certificate of diligent search is issued indicating that no one has claimed paternity. That certificate will be used by a judge to render a decision as to whether or not a putative father's parental rights should and can be terminated. It is important to note that some states will permit other forms of claims for paternity which would be a substitute for registering in a putative father registry. Check your state's requirements.

The Final Hearing

Finally, after a lengthy time of frustration, anxiety, and excitement, the day arrives for the adoption to be finalized in court. To the adoptive family, court employees, and the judge, this day brings joy and celebration. It's one of only a small handful of happy proceedings that regularly take place in a courthouse.

Our experience has been that the adoptive families bring friends and family to the final hearing, which without the consent of the family would otherwise be prohibited as it is a confidential and private proceeding. The hearing itself is a pretty routine event with the family confirming, under oath, that they understand their legal rights, duties, and responsibilities with respect to the child being adopted including the following:

- That the child is to be treated as a family would treat a biological child with no regard to the fact that the child is adopted
- That in the event the parents become divorced or separated, the issues of child support, custody, visitation, and other issues will be resolved in a manner no different from a divorce or separation involving a biological child
- That the child has all rights of inheritance under the state's inheritance laws as would a biological child

Typically, the judge will review the history contained in the court file and will execute a final judgment of adoption transferring legal custody of the child from the adoption entity to the parents, thus making the adoptive parents the legal parents of the child.

Another matter addressed at the final hearing of adoption is a review by the court of the expenses incurred by the prospective adoptive family for birth parent expenses (when permitted by law), agency and attorney's fees, court costs, and such other costs and expenses as are permitted by the state's adoption law. It is customary and sometimes legally required for the judge to sign an order approving the expenditure of funds to complete the adoption.

Once all of the above events are completed, the attorney will typically file an application with the state's office of vital statistics to secure a new birth certificate. The new birth certificate will have the child's new family name on it. The family can then apply for a Social Security number for the child. The process is now over!

Adoptive Family Filings

The documents which are typically filed in court for the prospective adoptive family are (i) the home study which must comply with state law; (ii) any agreement entered into between the family and the agency or attorney which lists, among other things, the willingness of the family to care for an adopted child, the projected fees and expenses associated with the adoption, the rights, duties, and responsibilities as well as the obligations of each party to the other as well as what happens if one party fails to comply with the contractual provisions; and (iii) the postplacement reports prepared by a licensed social worker after the child is placed in the prospective adoptive family's home but before the final hearing on the adoption.

The home study was already described in some detail elsewhere in this book.

As to the agreement between the family and the agency, while each agency or attorney has a different format for engaging with the prospective adoptive family, it is likely that such agreements include the following provisions in one form or another:

- That the agency, attorney, or social worker on the case expresses confidence in the family's ability to meet the social, familial, medical, and financial needs of a child
- That the family is willing and able to cooperate with the adoption process
- That the family's expectations regarding the adoption process are realistic and reflect the positives and negatives which are possible
- That the family is willing to assume the risks associated with the adoption process

- That the agency or attorney, if state law provides, will be the child's legal guardian until the adoption is finalized or until the court orders otherwise
- That the agency or attorney can remove the child from the family before the adoption is finalized, if it deems such a removal necessary to protect the child and that removal from the family is in the child's best interests
- That the payment of permitted expenses for the birth mother during and, perhaps, shortly after the pregnancy, does not guarantee that the adoption will be successfully completed
- That an agreed-upon representative will, prior to the completion of the adoption, prepare a final home study and prepare and file with the agency or attorney periodic reports as to the baby's and the family's progress on a postplacement basis and that the finalization of the adoption depends upon the agency and attorneys and court's acceptance and approval of such reports
- That the family will place the child under the care of a pediatrician promptly after the baby is discharged from the hospital and that such pediatric reports will be provided to the agency or attorney to enable them to make a decision regarding recommendation for finalization of the adoption
- That the family will notify the legal guardian of any serious illness or accident involving the child and secure the legal guardian's consent to any surgery required unless performed on an emergency basis
- That the family will notify the agency or attorney of any significant changes in the family's dynamics, including new address, new employment, or new member of the family
- That the family agrees to provide pictures and update letters at reasonable intervals per any agreement they have with the agency
- That the family will prepare a will or other legal document to appoint a guardian of the child should the child be without parents for any reason (i.e., death), after the adoption has been finalized

APPENDIX

B

Birth Parent(s) Legal Papers

The list below describes some of the information collected from and signed by the birth parents before the baby is born and which may be filed with the initial court filing to notify the court of the circumstances surrounding the proposed adoption:

- A disclosure form identifying the general rights of the birth parents under applicable state law and a statement indicating that the birth parents have received such disclosure. This document, known in Florida as the Adoption Disclosure Form, is the "bible" of the parties' rights and should be read and discussed very carefully.

- A genetic history and background information questionnaire detailing the background of the birth mother (and, where known and available, the birth father), including the medical histories of all children, parents, brothers, sisters, grandparents, and other relatives. The information gathered is intended to reveal to the prospective adoptive family the history of the birth parent(s) from ethnic, racial, medical, educational, occupational, legal, and social perspectives. This will also include information such as allergies, medical conditions, addictions, social, emotional, psychiatric, and similar conditions. It may also include the goals of the birth parent(s), their reason for contemplating adoption, recent employment, arrests, and other information which may be helpful for the family to know as the child grows up.

- A disclosure as to whether the birth mother is married or was cohabiting at the time she became pregnant and any and all details surrounding this issue should be documented. In this regard, it is not uncommon for a birth mother to be legally married but her husband is not the biological father of the pregnancy. In many cases the birth mother may not have had physical contact with or have even seen her husband in many years. Under some laws, however, the husband, who is not the biological father of the baby, is considered to be the "legal father" of the baby. No doubt this appears strange but the law favors that whenever possible, a child should have a "legal father" and not technically be born out of wedlock. Of course this set of facts initiates a series of legal events designed to be certain that the rights of all of the appropriate parties are terminated when that phase of the adoption process arrives.

- A disclosure stating whether either of the birth parents has any Native American Indian heritage. If so, a federal law known as the Indian Child Welfare Act of 1980 applies and any child who is a member of an Indian tribe or is eligible for membership in an Indian tribe or is the biological child of a member of an Indian tribe is considered to be an Indian child. Thus, the child is not free to be adopted by a non-Indian family unless specific steps have been taken to comply with the federal law or a waiver from the tribe is received. The essence of the law is that it is deemed desirable that a child with Indian heritage be placed with a member of the child's extended family as defined by the applicable tribe or, alternatively, another Indian family in order to protect the best interest of Indian children and to promote the security and stability of Indian tribes.

- There are multiple possibilities when dealing with an unknown birth father. The birth mother may not know who he is as a result of a sexual assault, a one-night stand, or some other encounter where names were unimportant (prostitution, escort services, etc.). If the birth mother states that she does not know who the birth father is, an inquiry should be made as to what she does know about him – ethnicity, race, physical description, and any other information she can provide. Not knowing who the birth father is influences the legal steps required to be taken to give a father constitutional rights to due process and notice of the prospective placement of the child for adoption.

In Florida, a search of the Florida Putative Father Registry is required to determine if the birth father has filed a claim of paternity with the State of Florida. If no claim is filed, his consent to the adoption may not be required. Alternatively, the birth mother may know or think she knows who the birth father is but refuse to identify him for personal reasons. He may be married to someone else and the birth mother doesn't want to disrupt his marriage, or he may pose a physical threat to her making her not want to identify him and thus avoid exposing herself to possible danger. Here again, we are faced with a situation where whoever he is, he is entitled to notice and due process but that cannot be accomplished in the conventional way if his identity is not disclosed. This man will be treated in the same manner as the completely unknown birth father.

Another scenario is the case where the birth mother knows and identifies who she believes is the father of the pregnancy. She discloses that information to the agency or its attorney and gives as complete a description of the person as is possible triggering a different course of action to either secure his consent, or the equivalent thereof, or take another action to attempt to prevent any effort he may make to interfere with the adoption if he is not cooperative. This known birth father is also required to register in the Putative Father Registry, and failure to do so may constitute a default which results in his consent becoming unnecessary to the termination of parental rights and adoption process. Any man who files a claim of paternity in the state's putative father registry will be notified of any legal action which will be taken to either terminate his parental rights or finalize an adoption of the child he is claimed to have fathered.

An effort must be made to locate the known birth father and serve him with court papers concerning the adoption and the termination of his parental rights. If he is locatable, he may have to be personally served; if he is not locatable after a diligent search is made, he may be served by publishing a notice in a local newspaper informing him of a forthcoming legal proceeding which involves his parental rights.

Other documents which are typically executed by birth parents include:

- A statement permitting the placement of the child for adoption with a family residing in a state other than the one in which the birth parent(s) resides
- A statement whereby the birth parents agree that the adoption case can be brought in a court not in the jurisdiction where they reside
- In states where permissible, a list of projected expenditures for the reasonable and necessary living expenses of the birth mother during, and sometimes for a short period of time after, the pregnancy as well as any other applicable expenditures permitted by the state's adoption law
- Of course the most important document required to be filed is the consent of the birth mother and, if available, the consent (or its equivalent known as an Affidavit of Nonpaternity) of the birth father. These documents must be signed, witnessed, and notarized before becoming enforceable. State laws determine at what times and under what circumstances the consent may be signed and strict adherence to those provisions of the law is critical.

"Safe Haven"

Some years ago there was a movement afoot throughout the United States to address the issue of women delivering babies and either murdering the babies or dumping them in a garbage can or dumpster. Although the problem wasn't widespread, each event was very notable due simply to its horrific nature and consequently received extraordinary local and national press coverage.

Some state legislatures responded with laws which were named (or nicknamed, depending on the jurisdiction) "safe haven" laws, indicating that a hospital or police station, for example, was a "safe haven" at which a person could drop an "unwanted" baby with no questions asked. The laws vary from state to state, of course, but the overall theory is the same.

Whether the law was successful, meaning whether it was able to achieve the stated goal of saving babies from being murdered or abandoned, depends on who you ask. In some states and jurisdictions, the application of the law can be flawed and sometimes skewed toward increasing the numbers to make it look more successful than it actually is. This can be done, for example, by encouraging women who might otherwise have chosen to voluntarily consent to adoption to leave the baby in the hospital instead, just so the placement can be considered a "safe haven" placement versus a voluntary adoption placement.

In Florida, as an example, there is no official organization responsible for implementing or tracking the statistics of Florida's safe haven laws. Various private organizations claim knowledge of or responsibility for keeping this information, but no official data-keeping entity has been designated by the law. Some of these organizations claim to "educate" law enforcement and other entities as to the existence of the law and the methods through which it's implemented, and hold elaborate fund raisers featuring locally important politicians and celebrities, all to raise money and "awareness" of a problem that was never really a widespread or pervasive problem.

Women still rarely, but from time to time, deliver and abandon babies. This law hasn't changed that. Some would argue that if all this law does is to save ONE baby it was worth it. We have an issue with the way some private entities are going about raising and using money in the name of this "one" proverbial baby. However, we commend these various entities for their tireless dedication to the children of the world, and acknowledge the great work they have done in this field. We do this (a) to commend the tireless efforts of fellow child advocates; and (b) because we don't want to be sued by them again.

As far as we can tell, we at One World Adoption Services did the first so-called "safe haven" placement in the State of Florida. We've only done a handful of these placements since the implementation of the law in 2000, because we believe the law is so flawed that we would rather not be on the hospitals' lists for that special call for a safe haven adoption. We would, nevertheless, provide the facilities and services to do such adoptions if called upon to do so as it is clearly a public interest issue and might well serve the best interests of the child who is the one being dropped off at a proper safe haven facility.

Why? Under Florida law, the woman who leaves the baby at a designated "safe haven" facility has until the termination of her parental rights to come back and reclaim the baby. Since the TPR (Termination of Parental Rights) hearing cannot be held for approximately 30 days after the entity takes custody of the baby, that amounts to a month of free babysitting for a woman who can't make up her mind as to whether or not to keep her baby.

> *Real-life example:* We received a call from a South Florida hospital that a baby girl had been brought in from a fire station where she had been left anonymously as a brand newborn, umbilical cord and all. The baby was discharged from the hospital to the care and custody of our agency which, in turn, placed the baby in the temporary care of a preadoptive family for hopeful subsequent adoption.
>
> We lawyers, on behalf of the agency, began conducting the necessary investigations as per Florida law. We checked with municipal, county, and state law enforcement, with The National Center for Missing and Exploited Children, and with the Florida Putative Father Registry, among others. Ultimately, we determined that absent a change of heart by the birth mother, the baby was free for adoption. The pleadings were prepared, the forms were filed, and the excited family was feeling extremely fortuitous.
>
> Eight days later, prior to being able to legally terminate the unknown mother's rights, the agency received a call from the uncle who was raising

the 19-year-old mother. The uncle advised that "no blood of his was being given up for no adoption." The uncle advised that he was sending his niece, the mother of the child, to court to reclaim her baby.

A hearing was held, the mother appeared and advised the judge that her uncle wanted her to keep the baby. The mother advised that she had no way of knowing who the father was, but did so with extreme indignation, as if it was deeply offensive to even ask the question. *This woman had the nerve, after dropping her newborn at a fire station and driving away, to suggest that the adoption agency was trying to "steal" her baby!*

A DNA test confirmed that this young woman was, indeed, the mother of the child. The judge ordered that the child be immediately transferred back to the care of the mother, case closed. The family who was caring for and hoping to permanently adopt this baby was nothing short of shattered.

NO, THANK YOU. We're not interested in doing that again.

Other Adoption Matters of Interest

Children with Special Needs

A child who the state has determined cannot or should not be returned to the home of his or her biological parents or a child who, because of some specific factor or condition (medical, emotional, mental, or physical), is often considered to be a child with "special needs" and will likely not be placed with an adoptive family without the family receiving some form of financial or other assistance from the state or federal government to enable the family to address the child's special needs. To get to that point, however, the state must have made a reasonable, albeit unsuccessful, effort to place the child with a family without the necessity of providing some form of financial assistance from the state.

As you can well imagine, the steps that must be completed to designate a child as having special needs are complicated, cumbersome, and very time-consuming. The benefits to the child and the family are, nevertheless, significant as they bring the child closer to being adopted by a stable family which can address his or her needs. The ultimate goal in a special needs adoption is to enable the child to have a much greater chance of a normal family structure in which to thrive. There are state and federal financial assistance programs to help families with the financial burdens often associated with the adoption of a child with special needs. This funding enables states to move children from state care to private care to provide the child with a forever-family environment in which to grow.

There are numerous benefits which are available to families which choose to adopt children with special needs in addition to the emotional rewards associated with essentially improving the likelihood that a child's life will be enhanced by his or her membership in a family. For example, children with special needs may well qualify for state and federal cash benefits to assist the adoptive family in providing for the needs of the child. The actual amount will be determined by the parameters of state and federal programs as well as the specific financial circumstances in which the prospective adoptive family finds itself. Oftentimes the amount of cash assistance given to a qualifying family will be comparable to the sum the state would otherwise have had to pay for foster care. These amounts may also be influenced by the amount of services required by the child as a result of specialized care which the child with special needs requires.

Many families adopting a child with special needs will also be eligible for other benefits such as federal and state tax credits, medical assistance, counseling, and other forms of social services and therapies including, in some instances, significant educational benefits such as tuition at state schools or at vocational schools.

Each case is different, and each requires an experienced advocate for the child's interests. The state will frequently pay for legal fees, court costs, home study fees, postplacement fees, and other expenses associated with the processing of the proposed adoption of a child with special needs.

States, along with the federal government, clearly recognize the need to provide many services as well as financial assistance to enable families to adopt children with special needs and help those children become productive members of society and well-rounded family members. Families that adopt children with special needs generally feel a sense of emotional fulfillment, which is often difficult to put into words.

Index

About the Authors

Robert A. Kasky, Esq., completed his first adoption in 1973 and has been involved in about 2,000 adoptions since then. Robert resides in South Florida with his wife of almost fifty years, Nancy.

Jeffrey A. Kasky, Esq., completed his last adoption in November of 2015 and is currently the President of The Autism Channel, Inc. (www.theautismchannel.tv). Jeff has been working in the field of major event risk management since 2005 and works as a fully-certified volunteer police officer in his spare time. Jeff enjoys working in the field of surrogacy so much that he, along with Marla Neufeld, Esq., is co-author of the upcoming title *The ABA Consumer Guide to Surrogacy: Techniques, Legal Issues, and Pathways to Success.*

Robert and Jeff are co-authors of the 2012 title *99 Things You Wish You Knew Before . . . Choosing Adoption.*

Robert and Jeff both love speaking to groups who are interested in adoption and/or surrogacy and are thus available for personal appearances. E-mail and inquiries should be directed to info@kaskymediation.com.